CW00486050

THE TASTE OF FREEDOM

Also by Sangharakshita

A Survey of Buddhism
A Guide to the Buddhist Path
The Three Jewels
The Essence of Zen
Peace is a Fire
Human Enlightenment
The Religion of Art
The Eternal Legacy
Travel Letters
Alternative Traditions
Who is the Buddha?
Ambedkar and Buddhism
Crossing The Stream
The History of My Going for Refuge
Flame in Darkness
The Ten Pillars of Buddhism
Vision and Transformation
New Currents in Western Buddhism
Learning to Walk *(memoirs)*
The Thousand-Petalled Lotus *(memoirs)*
In the Sign of the Golden Wheel *(memoirs)*
The Inconceivable Emancipation
Ritual and Devotion in Buddhism

The Buddha's Victory
Facing Mount Kanchenjunga *(memoirs)*
The Priceless Jewel
The Drama of Cosmic Enlightenment
The FWBO and 'Protestant Buddhism'
Wisdom Beyond Words
Forty-Three Years Ago
The Meaning of Conversion in Buddhism
Complete Poems 1941–1994
Was the Buddha a Bhikkhu?
In the Realm of the Lotus
Transforming Self and World
Buddhism for Today – and Tomorrow
Tibetan Buddhism: An Introduction

Booklets

Going for Refuge
Buddhism and the West
Great Buddhists of the Twentieth Century
The Meaning of Orthodoxy in Buddhism
Extending the Hand of Fellowship
My Relation to the Order
Mind – Reactive and Creative

SANGHARAKSHITA

THE TASTE OF FREEDOM

APPROACHES TO THE BUDDHIST PATH

WINDHORSE PUBLICATIONS

Published by Windhorse Publications
11 Park Road, Birmingham, B13 8AB
© Sangharakshita 1990
First published 1990
Second edition 1997

Printed by Interprint Ltd
Marsa, Malta
Cover design: Dhammarati
The front cover picture shows the dakini Vajravarahi, reproduced courtesy of Tiratanaloka
Other cover image © Photodisk

British Library Cataloguing in Publication Data:
A catalogue record for this book is available from the British Library.
ISBN 0 904766 90 x
(First edition 0 904766 42 x)

Since this work is intended for a general readership, Pali and Sanskrit words have been transliterated without the diacritical marks which would have been appropriate in a work of a more scholarly nature.

CONTENTS

ABOUT THE AUTHOR

SANGHARAKSHITA WAS BORN Dennis Lingwood in South London, in 1925. Largely self-educated, he developed an interest in the cultures and philosophies of the East early on, and realized that he was a Buddhist at the age of sixteen.

The Second World War took him, as a conscript, to India, where he stayed on to become the Buddhist monk Sangharakshita ('protected by the spiritual community'). After studying for some years under leading teachers from the major Buddhist traditions, he went on to teach and write extensively. He also played a key part in the revival of Buddhism in India, particularly through his work among the ex-Untouchables.

After twenty years in India, he returned to England to establish the Friends of the Western Buddhist Order (FWBO) in 1967, and the Western Buddhist Order (called Trailokya Bauddha Mahasangha in India) in 1968. A translator between East and West, between the traditional world and the modern, between principles and practices, Sangharakshita's depth of experience and clear thinking have been appreciated throughout the world. He has always particularly emphasized the decisive significance of commitment in the spiritual life, the paramount value of spiritual friendship and community, the link between religion and art, and the need for a 'new society' supportive of spiritual aspirations and ideals.

The FWBO is now an international Buddhist movement with centres in sixteen countries worldwide. In recent years Sangharakshita has been handing on most of his responsibilities to his senior disciples in the Order. From his base in London, he is now focusing on personal contact with people, and on his writing.

INTRODUCTION

A QUAINT MEMORY still haunts me from the mid-nineteen-seventies. I am attending a Buddhist 'summer school' somewhere in the English countryside just outside London. Our days are filled with study groups, talks, chance meetings in the landscaped grounds, and demonstrations of yoga, flower arranging, and karate. There is also just a little meditation practice. The talks and study groups run from Theravada to Zen, through Zoroastrianism and Vedanta, to a sort of bizarre synthesis of ancient and modern teachings, whose pundit encourages his disciples to spend substantial periods of time with paper bags over their heads.

Each evening we are treated to a formal lecture. For an hour or so our minds are crammed with scholarly detail, dazzled by koans, or titillated by the intimate reminiscences of those who have sat at the feet of Great Masters. This is the climactic event of the day: dress is formal and the air in the lecture room hangs heavy with the scent, not of incense, but of ladies' perfume. A handful of monks have graced our gathering with their presence, and as they enter the room – always at the last moment – to take their place at the front, the assembly rises and, in the awkward unison of people who left school more years ago than they care to recall, bows rigidly.

On one particular evening the monks are later than usual; the atmosphere is growing discreetly restive. The door then opens to reveal an informally dressed, and rather abashed, sixteen-year-old. This young man, I have already discovered, is with us because he is spending his school holidays with some Buddhistically-inclined friends of his parents, and has tagged along as a matter of course. He shows little interest in the programme, and spends most of his time out on the estate's miniature golf-course. Nevertheless, his sudden and unavoidably prominent entry into the room provokes a tangible tremor of confusion in our ranks. Uncertainly at first, a few people rise to their feet – followed a little raggedly by the rest – join their hands at the palms, and offer the boy a salutation. He tries to smile away his embarrassment, and scurries for the first seat he can find. You see, he comes from Thailand, and in this setting nobody seems to be quite sure what is and what is not deserving of reverence.

For me that memory characterizes an era of Western Buddhism that was, even then, mercifully coming to an end. A year later that same summer school was revamped so as to attract people more interested in Buddhism as a set of practical teachings than as a chaotic jumble of exciting and exotic mental games. But it was into this earlier Western Buddhist scene, this heady if fruitless mix of *shunya*-babble, *do*-talk, arguments about the relative 'orthodoxy' of the most superficially understood views, small-group politics, and generalized confusion, that the Venerable Sangharakshita had fairly recently arrived from the East. And it was during this transitional era in the development of Western Buddhism that he gave the talks which, in lightly edited form, make up this book.

By that time Sangharakshita's greatest contribution to the transformation of the Buddhist world had been his founding of the Friends of the Western Buddhist Order in 1967, and of the Western Buddhist Order itself in 1968. His original intention had been to make a brief contribution through existing channels. However, led to some extent by circumstances, he had found himself abandoning his life in India where he had friends, literary projects, a vihara to run, and a crucial part to play in Dr Ambedkar's Buddhist 'conversion' movement, to create an entirely new Buddhist community – indeed a new *kind* of Buddhist community – among his fellow Westerners.

By the mid-seventies that community could be described as a movement, and involved, perhaps, a thousand people at its periphery, and a couple of hundred at its core. There were public Dharma centres in London, Glasgow, Brighton, Manchester, and Norwich in the UK, and burgeoning outposts in Finland and New Zealand, all run by members of the Order. It was also becoming increasingly multidimensional as people discovered that their involvement with the movement, and thus with Buddhism, could extend beyond attendance at evening classes and occasional retreats to include community living, cooperative business ventures, indeed an entire way of life based on Buddhist values and practice. Suddenly it was becoming possible to commit not just one's mind, but one's life, to Buddhism. For those of us involved at the time, life lived as a Buddhist was exciting. But it was also lovely.

The real key to the FWBO's gathering momentum and relative success was not so much the tribal enthusiasm of a tightly-knit group of mainly young people – though that element cannot be ignored (nor was it by the movement's critics) – but the almost tangible connection we felt with a coherent vision of the Buddhist ideal and the Buddhist path. We knew what we were doing: we could see how the Buddhist teachings fitted together and how they could be used to power and direct the affairs of everyday life. Certainly, Buddhism came alive in the meditation hall and on the country retreat; it always had. But now we were bringing it into our business meetings, on to the building sites of our new centres, tossing it around the breakfast table, and ushering it into the work environment, not as a set of platitudinous safety valves for warding off boredom, frustration, anger, or over-worldliness, but as an increasingly implicit guiding force that could saturate every action, every debate, and, if necessary, every argument. We were really *doing* it.

But we were doing it differently. Our very vision of the Dharma was a new – if radical – synthesis, the creative achievement of a teacher who had immersed himself, somewhat controversially, in not one but all of Buddhism's major strands. And that teacher was himself a problematic figure. He was ordained as, and sometimes wore the robes of, a Theravadin bhikkhu, or 'monk', but was well known for his critical views on the state of the contemporary Theravada world, and for his obvious espousal of Mahayana ideals and practices. The members of his Order observed a clear set of ethical precepts; and many of them were now full-time Dharma workers. But with no fixed rules and no defined lifestyle they were regarded as 'lay followers'. In traditional terms, a Buddhist movement without monks or nuns hardly counted for anything; yet, here we were, practising meditation, immersing ourselves in the suttas and sutras, offering classes, building centres, establishing a viable economic base, creating an entire Buddhist movement, while the rest of the Western Buddhist world seemed to be largely preoccupied with the plight of geese trapped in bottles.

All this was about to change. The coming years would see the emergence into greater prominence of the Manjushri Institute, Throssel Hole Priory, Chögyam Trungpa's Dharmadhatu network, Tarthang Tulku's Nyingma movement, and a number of other organizations dedicated to committed Dharma practice. The FWBO would remain unique for a while to the extent that it sought to present the Dharma in Western dress; it is still unique in its emphasis on the supremacy of the Going for Refuge – the act of *commitment* to Buddhist ideals and practice – over lifestyle; but it would no longer be alone in offering the sole opportunity in the UK, and perhaps in the West, for an entirely Buddhist way of life.

And so the chapters that follow have a twofold value today. Firstly, they each stand alone, and intact, as they did in their original form as excellent Dharma-talks, revealing both the depth and breadth of Sangharakshita's grasp of Buddhism, and providing a clear testament to his skills as a 'translator' of Buddhist terms and teachings for a new audience in a new age. In that they are expressions of the Buddha-Dharma they are as relevant to us now as they ever were. No matter how far we have come, no matter how long we have been practising, nor in what context, we each need to clarify – each day afresh – our ideas about the path we are treading, and the goal towards which we are heading.

But, secondly, this book serves also as a series of time-capsules, revealing how people saw Buddhism – or failed to see it – just a little while ago. Two of the talks, 'The Path of Regular Steps and the Path of Irregular Steps' and 'Enlightenment as Experience and as Non-experience', were given under the auspices of the London Buddhist Society – which we precocious tyros rather unfairly viewed as the very Mordor of the Buddhist world (while it possibly regarded us as something worse) – with the legendary Christmas Humphreys in the chair. Perhaps the time has come to admit that many of us who attended those evenings (ostentatiously dressing down for the occasion) were inwardly cheering on our unlikely champion, him of the deliberate inflexions and the almost tortuously precise sentences, hoping that he would, in his characteristically genteel way, gloriously show 'them' what was what.

But that was not, and never has been, his way. Our expectations did no justice to his intentions. True, there were a few gentle digs, some oblique, almost hidden, references to past differences, and a confident assertion of the FWBO's unique significance, which gave some cheer to the gallery. But the fact remained that we, for all our towering self-assurance, had also to make the move from the path of irregular steps to the path of regular steps; we too had to learn to think of Enlightenment as non-experience rather than as experience. Really we had barely started. Reviewing those talks after so many years, and feeling their relevance to my own spiritual life as much as ever, I marvel that his closest friends could not see how, in speaking to the Buddhist world, Sangharakshita was also speaking very directly to us.

Walking around Caxton Hall just before one of the talks began, I happened upon someone whom I knew to be centrally involved in the creation of a major Tibetan Buddhist centre. When I confessed my surprise at seeing him there, he seemed baffled, and said 'But Sangharakshita is a teacher for all Western Dharma practitioners.'

He was right and, in a way, I was wrong. Sangharakshita was not just *our* teacher; he was, and is, a teacher for anyone in the modern world who wishes to know what Buddhism, stripped of its exotic cultural accretions, is actually saying to us. In this little book there is enough information and enough wisdom not only to cut through the confusion that must inevitably assail the hapless newcomer to the vast forest of Buddhism, but to place that newcomer – along with us not-so-old-timers – on the path of vision and transformation that will lead us, in time, to freedom.

Nagabodhi
Vimalakula Community
November 1989

EDITOR'S NOTE: In order to bring this volume into line with other more recently edited lectures and seminars given by Sangharakshita, these talks have been further edited to take closer account of the literary medium in which they are now presented. At the same time we hope that their origin as a series of talks given on particular occasions will still be amply discernible.

Jinananda
Spoken Word Project
West London Buddhist Centre
March 1997

THE TASTE OF FREEDOM

WHAT IS BUDDHISM? Over the years there have been quite a number of attempts to answer this question, or to define this protean term. Buddhism has been defined as a code or system of ethics, as an Eastern philosophy, and even as a form of Eastern mysticism. It has been described as a spiritual path and as a tradition. By some people, on at least some occasions, it has even been described as a religion. Worse still, for the last hundred or so years it has been described as 'Buddhism'. Until that time what we nowadays call Buddhism was known simply as the *Dharma* or, more precisely, as the *Dharma-Vinaya*: the principle and the practice.

But going back to the beginning, we find that it was the Buddha himself who gave us the best definition – or at least the best description – of Buddhism. And he gave it in the form of an image rather than in terms of concepts or abstract ideas. The Buddha simply said that Buddhism, or the Dharma-Vinaya, was an ocean, a great and mighty ocean.

This description occurs in a Pali text: the *Udana* or 'Verses of Uplift'. The *Udana* tells us that one full moon night the Buddha was seated surrounded by a great number of what the text calls *bhikkhus*. This word is usually translated, in its singular form, as 'monk' or 'brother', but is perhaps better translated as 'partaker', the bhikkhu being one who partakes of, or shares in, the food of the land in the form of his daily alms, as well as one who partakes of, or shares in, the spiritual life along with the Buddha and his fellow disciples. Thus the Buddha was seated surrounded by a great number of partakers. According to the *Udana*, they all sat there together, in complete silence, not just for one or two hours, but for the whole night. They didn't say a word. They didn't fidget. They didn't even blow their noses. One could say they meditated together, but perhaps they were all at a stage where you don't even need to meditate. You simply sit there – all night.

Then, just as dawn was about to break, something happened. I won't go into the full story, but it transpired that one of those present, though professing to be committed to the spiritual life, was in fact 'unvirtuous, wicked, unclean, of suspect habits, secretive of his acts, no monk but claiming to be one'. Maha-Moggallana, who among all the Buddha's disciples was known for the accuracy of his intuition, became aware of this man's true nature, and prevailed upon him to leave. And it was with reference to this incident that the Buddha described the Dharma-Vinaya in terms of the 'mighty ocean'. There were eight strange and wonderful things about the mighty ocean, he said, and similarly there were eight strange and wonderful things about the Dharma-Vinaya.

THE EIGHT STRANGE AND WONDERFUL THINGS

Firstly, the mighty ocean gets deeper little by little. We are to imagine, it seems, a gradually sloping shore, not a coastline of sheer cliffs dropping suddenly into the sea. Similarly, the training, the course, the path, of the Dharma-Vinaya is gradual. There is no abrupt penetration of knowledge. The path is – as we shall see in the next chapter – a path of regular steps.

Secondly, the Buddha said, the mighty ocean is 'of a stable nature, not overpassing its boundary'. Just so, the Buddha's disciples do not transgress, even for the sake of life itself, the training he has enjoined on them. In more familiar terms, the commitment of the Buddha's disciples to the Dharma-Vinaya is absolute.

Thirdly, the mighty ocean 'does not associate with a dead body but casts it up on to the shore'. In the same way, the sangha or spiritual community of the Buddha's disciples rejects one who is not, in fact, leading a spiritual life, though outwardly professing to do so. Even though seated in the midst of the sangha such a person is far from the sangha, and the sangha is far from him. This, of course, is a reference to what has just happened. In other words, there is no such thing as nominal membership of the spiritual community. There is no such thing as honorary membership. Sooner or later, therefore, a nominal member will have to 'leave', or rather, as the bogus 'partaker' did, simply find himself or herself outside.

Fourthly, when great rivers reach the mighty ocean they abandon their former names and lineage, and instead of being known as the Ganges, the Jumna, and so on, are reckoned simply as 'mighty ocean'. In the same way those who 'go forth' from home into the homeless life in response to the Dharma-Vinaya proclaimed by the Buddha lose their former names and lineage and are reckoned simply as 'ascetics who are sons of the Shakyan', that is to say, ascetics who are disciples or followers of the Buddha. In other words, they become part of the spiritual community – or, to put it more precisely, they are 'merged' with the spiritual community without losing their individual spiritual identity.

The Buddha himself spoke in terms of abandoning one's *caste* identity as a noble, a brahmin, a merchant, or a serf – those being the four main hereditary castes of his day. But we in the West must think in rather different terms. We can speak, for example, of abandoning our national identity. Within the spiritual community there is no question of being English or Irish or Scottish or Welsh, no question of being American or Indian or Australian or Finnish or Dutch. Within the spiritual community one is simply a spiritually committed human being, relating as such to other spiritually committed human beings.

Fifthly, whatever streams flow into the mighty ocean, or whatever rains fall from the sky, the mighty ocean neither increases nor decreases. This is not strictly true, of course: in the Buddha's day people did not, it seems, know anything about the polar ice caps. However, that does not really matter. The important thing is not the scientific accuracy of the comparison, but the point it is meant to illustrate. If we can imagine that the mighty ocean neither increases nor decreases, then we can say that, similarly, though many people pass finally away into that condition of nirvana which 'leaves nothing behind', yet that condition of nirvana neither increases nor decreases.

Sixthly, the mighty ocean has one taste, the taste of salt. Just so, the Dharma-Vinaya has one taste, the taste of freedom.

Seventhly, the mighty ocean contains many kinds of gems. As the poet Gray puts it in his 'Elegy in a Country Churchyard':

Full many a gem of purest ray serene
The dark unfathom'd caves of ocean bear.

Similarly, the Dharma-Vinaya contains many kinds of spiritual teachings, such as the four foundations of mindfulness, the five spiritual faculties, the seven factors of Enlightenment, the Noble Eightfold Path, and so on.

Eighthly and lastly, the mighty ocean is the abode of monsters such as the leviathan, the fisheater, and so on. Here the *Udana* seems to be a little uncertain about its marine biology, but evidently creatures like whales and sharks are meant, besides creatures of a more fabulous kind. Whatever they are, the mighty ocean is their abode. In the same way, the Dharma-Vinaya is the abode of great beings such as Stream-entrants, once-returners, non-returners, and arahants. It is also the abode, we could add (though the *Udana* does not actually say so), of bodhisattvas and maha-siddhas, gurus and devas, dakas and dakinis and dharmapalas.

Thus there are these eight strange and wonderful things about the mighty ocean, and these eight strange and wonderful things about the Dharma-Vinaya. And of these eight things we are here going to be focusing on the sixth, on the fact that the Dharma-Vinaya, or what we have got into the habit – unfortunately – of calling Buddhism, has 'the taste of freedom'. But before doing so, let us pause for a moment over something that we might easily overlook in the Buddha's description of the Dharma-Vinaya as being like the mighty ocean. We need to allow these two epithets – 'strange' and 'wonderful' – to have their full effect on us.

In what sense is the mighty ocean strange? Here we must remember that the Buddha lived and taught in the valley of the Ganges, many hundreds of miles from the sea. So far as we know, he had never seen the mighty ocean, and the vast majority of his disciples had never seen it either. They had probably simply heard a rumour to the effect that far beyond their own land there existed a great body of water far greater than any river, greater even than the Ganges itself. So to them the mighty ocean was a foreign, an unfamiliar, element.

It was the same – it *is* the same – in the case of the Dharma-Vinaya. The Dharma-Vinaya is strange to us. We can in fact go further and say that the spiritual life is strange to us; the unconditioned is strange to us; the transcendental is strange to us. It is something of which we have only heard. It is foreign to us; it is not our native element. Indeed, the Buddha himself is strange to us. He is a stranger in an ultimate sense. He comes from another world, another dimension, as it were. He stands at our door, perhaps, but we do not recognize him. Even the spiritual community is strange to us if we are not ourselves true individuals, or are not spiritually committed. Thus the mighty ocean of the Dharma-Vinaya is strange to us.

But in what sense is the mighty ocean wonderful? It is wonderful in its vast extent. It is wonderful in its perpetual movement: it never rests, not even for a moment, not even the tiniest particle of it. It is wonderful in its uninterrupted music: 'the sound of the ocean tide'. It is wonderful in its ever-changing lights and colours: the blue and the green and the mauve; the purple, the gold. It is wonderful in its unfathomable depth. It is particularly wonderful when we see it, and come into contact with it, and perhaps swim in it, when we plunge in, move our arms and legs about and, perhaps for the first time in our lives, find that we are swimming in the mighty ocean. Or at least, if we haven't summoned the nerve to take the plunge, we can at least paddle, feeling the force of the waves, looking in wonder towards the horizon where sea meets sky.

It is the same with the Dharma-Vinaya, except that the Dharma-Vinaya is not simply vast; it is infinite. The Dharma-Vinaya – the principle and the practice of the Dharma – is a shoreless ocean. We can see no end to it. And it is not fixed, rigid, static, unmoving, unchanging, but full of life, full of movement. It is continually adapting itself to the needs of living beings, continually speaking to us, singing to us, playing its own inimitable music to us, in its own indescribably appealing and fascinating way. It is no dull religious monument; it is alive with all sorts of brilliant and tender lights, all sorts of vivid and delicate colours. It is alive with the radiantly colourful forms of Buddhas and bodhisattvas, dakas and dakinis. And it is so deep, this mighty ocean of the Dharma-Vinaya, that we can never hope to fathom it. The Dharma-Vinaya is wonderful in all these ways.

Perhaps we don't usually think of the Dharma-Vinaya in this manner; but this is what it is really like. It is wonderful. The Buddha is wonderful. As Matricheta says in his 'Five Hundred Verses of Worship':

> *What steadfastness! What conduct! What form! What virtues!*
> *In a Buddha's attributes there is nothing that is not wonderful.*

The spiritual community is wonderful. Spiritual life is wonderful. It is wonderful that we can sit and meditate together. It is wonderful that we can live in residential spiritual communities. It is wonderful that we can work in right livelihood projects. It is wonderful that I am able to speak to you in this way. It is wonderful that what I am communicating in the form of a talk can be metamorphosed by editors into the chapter of a book. It is wonderful that you are reading this book now. Thus the Dharma-Vinaya is indeed wonderful: strange and wonderful.

Perhaps this is how we experience the Dharma-Vinaya when we first come across it, and we might think that we will never forget how wonderful it is. But after a while, I'm sorry to say, we are only too likely to start experiencing Buddhism – or spiritual life – as 'old hat': a stage we went through when we were young and naïve, but which we have long since outgrown. It is said that familiarity breeds contempt, but it is probably more true to say that familiarity breeds indifference.

Of course, in the case of the Dharma-Vinaya, the familiarity that breeds contempt is usually with the words, concepts, and external forms in which it finds expression. But the Dharma-Vinaya is not to be identified with its external forms. And if we become familiar with the *spirit* of the Dharma-Vinaya, or even have a tongue-tip taste of it, we will see the Dharma-Vinaya as more and more wonderful. It is important to keep alive this sense that the Dharma-Vinaya is a wonderful thing; and thus at the same time keep alive a sense of the spirit of the Dharma-Vinaya. According to Plato, philosophy begins with a sense of wonder; and certainly there is no spiritual life without an ever-continuing sense of wonder.

But we can go further than that – and in the *Udana* the Buddha does so. The *Udana* goes further than that. After describing the eight strange and wonderful qualities of the Dharma-Vinaya, the Buddha says 'These, then, partakers, are the eight strange and wonderful things in this Dharma-Vinaya, beholding which again and again partakers take delight in this Dharma-Vinaya.'

Here again we find a couple of very significant expressions. Firstly, just as some people see a film again and again without ever becoming tired of it, so the partakers – that is, the followers of the Buddha – see the Dharma-Vinaya, look at the Dharma-Vinaya, hear the Dharma-Vinaya, without ever becoming tired of it. In fact the more they see and hear of the Dharma-Vinaya the more wonderful it appears.

Secondly, the partakers take delight in the Dharma-Vinaya. The Dharma-Vinaya is not only wonderful but also enjoyable. It is enjoyable because it is wonderful. It is wonderful because it is enjoyable. Spiritual life is enjoyable. Meditation is enjoyable. Living in a residential spiritual community is enjoyable. Working in a right livelihood project is enjoyable. Being 'thrown in at the deep end' is enjoyable. Not being allowed to rationalize away our slips and failings is enjoyable. It is important to remember this: that in every way the Dharma-Vinaya is enjoyable. Buddhism is enjoyable. It is something in which, seeing it again and again, we take delight. It is hardly necessary to point out how greatly this differs from the usual conception of religion and religious life.

And of all the strange and wonderful qualities of the Dharma-Vinaya, I want now to focus on one in particular: that it has the taste of freedom.

WHAT IS FREEDOM?

This is perhaps a question that we ask ourselves even more often than we ask 'What is Buddhism?' and the answer for most of us will have, probably, something to do with civil and political liberties. However, the concept we are dealing with here is expressed by another word altogether, of which 'freedom' is just a translation. This is the Pali term *vimutti* (Sanskrit *vimukti*), which translates as 'release', 'emancipation', or 'freedom'. Thus we are concerned not with the meaning of the English word, as such, but only with its meaning as a provisional equivalent of the original Pali term. We are concerned with freedom in the sense of *vimutti*, not with *vimutti* in the sense of freedom.

What, then, is *vimutti*? In order to begin to understand this we shall have to see what place *vimutti* occupies in the complete scheme of spiritual self-development; and we can do this by looking at where it comes in the series of the 'positive' *nidanas*, as I have called them.

These *nidanas* represent stages of spiritual development. They are called *nidanas* or 'links' because each one arises in dependence on the one preceding or, we may say, out of the fullness of the one preceding. Thus in dependence on suffering arises faith and devotion; in dependence on faith and devotion arises satisfaction and delight; in dependence on satisfaction and delight arises rapture; in dependence on rapture arises tranquillity; in dependence on tranquillity arises bliss; in dependence on bliss arises *samadhi* or 'concentration' – in the sense not of mere mental concentration, but of the complete integration of all the psychophysical energies of one's being; in dependence on *samadhi* arises knowledge and vision of things as they really are; in dependence on knowledge and vision of things as they really are arises disengagement, or disentanglement; in dependence on disengagement, or disentanglement, arises dispassion; in dependence on dispassion arises *vimutti*; in dependence on *vimutti* arises knowledge of the destruction of the 'biases' (craving, wrong views, and ignorance).

And this is the last of the twelve positive *nidanas*, for knowledge of the destruction of the biases is equivalent to Enlightenment, representing the goal and consummation of the entire spiritual life, as well as the complete overcoming of mundane existence, and, by implication, the complete realization of the unconditioned and transcendental.

This is not the place for a detailed account of this progressive series. Simply listing them, however, makes one thing at least clear: that *vimutti* occupies a very high place indeed in the whole series, and thus in the complete scheme of spiritual self-development. It is, in fact, the penultimate stage. *Vimutti* is not, therefore, what we ordinarily understand by freedom: it goes far, far beyond that. It goes far beyond any question of political and civil liberties, and far beyond freedom in the ordinary psychological sense. But if this is so, then what are we to make of the term? Let us see if we can work our way towards a clearer impression of the nature of freedom in the sense of *vimutti*.

The fourth to the seventh *nidanas* – rapture, tranquillity, bliss, and *samadhi* – represent the process of what is usually called meditation, that is to say, meditation in the sense of an actual experience of higher states of consciousness, not meditation simply in the sense of preliminary concentration. They constitute meditation in the sense of what is technically called *samatha* or 'calm', and they are very considerable attainments indeed. But it is the next stage, 'knowledge and vision of things as they really are', that is the important one. In fact, the transition from *samadhi* to knowledge and vision of reality is absolutely crucial. It represents the great turning point in the spiritual life. It is the point at which our most refined, most blissful, most beatific experience of the conditioned, or of the mundane, is succeeded by the first 'experience' – there is no other word for us to use here – of the unconditioned, the transcendental. 'Knowledge and vision of things as they really are' thus constitutes a form of what is technically called *vipassana* or Insight.

The fact that *vimutti* occurs subsequent to knowledge and vision of things as they really are (with two other stages in between) means that there is no *vimutti* – no real freedom – without Insight. Moreover, when 'knowledge and vision of things as they really are' arises, and one makes that crucial transition from calm to Insight, one is said – in traditional Buddhist language – to 'enter the stream': one becomes a 'Stream-entrant', or – to use another traditional term – an *ariya-puggala* or 'true individual'. So freedom in the sense of *vimutti* is accessible only to one who has become a Stream-entrant, a true individual.

All this should establish unequivocally the scale of experience denoted by the term *vimutti*, or freedom. However, it may still leave us little the wiser as to the actual nature of *vimutti*. To begin to estimate this we need to look at that crucial point when we 'enter the stream'. What in fact happens as we do that, or as that happens to us – both these expressions here have the same meaning – is that we break free from (or there are broken) the first three 'fetters' binding us to the lower, grosser levels of mundane existence. It is the breaking of these fetters that will give us a real 'taste of freedom'.

These three fetters are usually described as: firstly, the fetter of belief in an essential, unchanging self; secondly, the fetter of doubt and indecision with regard to the Dharma; and thirdly, the fetter of attachment to religious observances as ends in themselves. Here, however, we are going to approach them in very general, even basic – or down-to-earth – terms, as: firstly, the fetter of *habit*; secondly, the fetter of *superficiality*; and thirdly, the fetter of *vagueness*.

THE FETTER OF HABIT

A habit is something we are said to *have*. We have 'the tendency or disposition to act in a particular way'. However, as this dictionary definition makes clear, a habit consists of actions, and action is an essential part of us, not just something added on, something we have. In fact according to the Dhamma-Vinaya we *are* our actions. And this is the way we usually think of, and refer to, a person: someone is the sum total of his or her actions of body, speech, and mind, and doesn't exist apart from these.

The fact that we have a 'tendency or disposition to *act* in a particular way' means, therefore, that we have a tendency or disposition to *be* in a particular way. We are not just the sum total of our actions: we are the sum total of our habits. We *are* our habits. We could even say that each one of us is simply a habit – probably a bad habit. The person we think of as George or Mary, and recognize as acting in a particular way, is simply a habit that a certain stream of consciousness has got into.

But since it has got into it, it can get out of it. It is like a knot tied in a piece of string: it can be untied. Breaking the fetter of habit means, essentially, getting out of the habit of being a particular kind of person. It is only a habit you have got into. You don't *have* to be the way you are. There is no necessity about it. Breaking the fetter of habit means, therefore, getting rid of the old self, the past self. It means becoming a true individual; that is, becoming continually aware and emotionally positive, continually responsible, sensitive, and creative – continually creative of one's own self.

This is the meaning of the Buddhist doctrine of *anatta* or 'no-self'. It is not so much that we never have a self as that we always have a *new* self. And if each new self is a better one than the last, then we can say that spiritual progress is taking place.

It is not easy to get out of the habit of being the kind of person that we are. It is not easy to get rid of the old self and become a true individual. One of the reasons for this is other people. Not only have we ourselves got into the habit of being in a particular way, but other people have got into the habit of experiencing us as being in the habit of being in a particular way.

The people who experience us as what we *were* rather than as what we *are* – or what we are in process of becoming – represent a collective way of thinking, feeling, and acting. They represent the group as opposed to the individual. The group is the enemy of the individual – of the true individual – inasmuch as it will not allow the true individual to emerge from its ranks. It insists on dealing with you not as you are but as you were, and to this extent it tries to deal with someone who no longer exists. This tends to happen, for example, when one visits one's family after some time.

Becoming free of the group does not, of course, necessarily mean actually breaking off relations with the group. What it means is breaking away from the influence – the habit-reinforcing influence – of the group.

THE FETTER OF SUPERFICIALITY

To be superficial means to act from the surface of ourselves and, in consequence, to act without thoroughness or care; it is about acting in outward appearance rather than genuinely or actually. Now why should we do this? Why should we act superficially?

The reason is that we are divided. More often than not, the conscious rational surface is divided from the unconscious emotional depths. We act out of intellectual conviction but do not succeed in carrying the emotions with us. Sometimes, of course, we do act out of the fullness of our emotions but then, only too often, the rational mind holds back, and even, perhaps, does not approve. In neither case do we act totally, wholeheartedly. We do not act with the whole of ourselves and, therefore, in a sense, do not really act at all.

This state of affairs is very general. Superficiality is one of the curses of the modern age. Matthew Arnold, more than a hundred years ago, spoke of our 'sick hurry', our 'divided aims' – and that just about describes the situation. We are neurotically busy, without any real focus, any singleness of purpose. We don't truly, authentically, do anything. We don't do anything with the whole force of our being. When we love we don't really love, and when we hate we don't really hate. We don't even really think. We half do all these things.

It is the same, only too often, when we take up the spiritual life and try to follow the Dharma-Vinaya. When we meditate, it is only with part of ourselves. When we communicate, or when we work, again it is only with part of ourselves. Consequently we don't get very far: we don't really grow; we don't really develop. We don't carry the whole of our being along with us, so to speak. A small part of us is prospecting ahead, but the greater part is lagging far behind.

Breaking the fetter of superficiality therefore means acting with the whole of oneself: acting with thoroughness and care; acting genuinely and actually. It means, in a word, commitment. It means committing oneself to the spiritual life, committing oneself to being a true individual.

THE FETTER OF VAGUENESS

'Vague' means 'indistinct, not clearly expressed or identified, of uncertain or ill-defined meaning or character'. So why should anyone *be* vague? The fact is, we are vague when we are un-decided, vague when we don't *want* to decide, and, above all, vague when we don't want to commit ourselves. Our vagueness is, therefore, a dishonest vagueness.

After all, spiritual life is very difficult. Growth and development is often a painful process (even though it is always enjoyable). Therefore we tend to shrink back. We keep our options open. We keep a number of different interests, or a number of different aims, on which we can fall back, and allow ourselves to oscillate between them, even to drift between them. At all costs we remain vague: woolly, foggy, shapeless, indistinct, unclear.

Breaking the fetter of vagueness means being willing to think clearly. It means giving time to thinking things out, having the determination to think things through. It means being prepared to look at what the alternatives really are, and to sort out one's priorities. It means being ready to make up one's mind. It means making a decision to choose the best and then to act wholeheart-edly upon that choice. It means not postponing the moment of decision.

TASTING THE TEACHINGS

The three fetters – of habit, of superficiality, and of vagueness – are broken by means of Insight, that is, by means of knowledge and vision of things as they really are. In less traditional terms, they are broken by our becoming creative (in the sense of self-creative or creative of our own new self), by becoming committed, and by becoming clear. When Insight arises, one enters the Stream, the Stream that leads directly to Enlightenment: one becomes a Stream-entrant and, being a Stream-entrant, one becomes a true individual. And as a true individual, one can experience *vimutti*, one can enjoy the taste of freedom.

Two key points emerge from all this. The first is that only the true individual is really free; the second, that one becomes a true individual only by developing Insight: that is, by breaking the three fetters and thereby becoming creative, committed, and clear. This is freedom.

So what does the Buddha mean by the *taste* of freedom? When the Buddha says 'Just as the mighty ocean has one taste, the taste of salt, so the Dharma-Vinaya has one taste, the taste of freedom' – what does this mean? It means, of course, what it says – that the Dharma-Vinaya is wholly pervaded by the taste of freedom. Every part of it has that taste.

The Dharma-Vinaya consists of a great many things – perhaps more now than in the Buddha's own day. It consists of all sorts of teachings, all sorts of practices, all sorts of institutions. It consists of philosophies, concentration techniques, ethical systems, rituals, arts – entire cultures, in fact. But the one question that must be asked about all these things is: do they have the taste of freedom? That is, do they help us, directly or indirectly, to become free in the sense of *vimutta*? Do they help us to develop Insight – i.e. to break the three fetters and 'enter the Stream' – and thus become true individuals? Because if they do not, then they form no part of the Buddha's teaching, no part of the Dharma-Vinaya.

It must be admitted that there are many things in the traditional practice of Buddhism in the East with regard to which we cannot answer these questions in the affirmative. Whether it is the Theravada, or Tibetan Buddhism, or Zen, there are many elements within these rich and important traditions that do not have this 'taste of freedom'. This is why we do not, in the Friends of the

Western Buddhist Order, identify ourselves exclusively with any one form of traditional Buddhism. Instead, we follow the Buddha's own advice and accept as his teaching only what helps us to grow, or what actually has the taste of freedom.

One issue raised by the title of this essay remains unaddressed. How is it that the Buddha speaks not of the *idea* or *concept* of freedom but of its *taste*? One could, of course, argue that he does this only because he has already spoken of the mighty ocean as having the taste of salt: that the word 'taste' is used literally when referring to the ocean, and only metaphorically with regard to freedom. However, it is in fact the ocean that is the metaphor, not the Dharma-Vinaya. He speaks of the taste of salt in order to emphasize a corresponding quality of the Dharma-Vinaya: that the Dharma-Vinaya likewise has its characteristic taste – the taste of freedom. He wants to emphasize that freedom is something to be tasted. So what is this really about?

The Pali term translated as 'taste' is *rasa*, which means 'juice, special quality, flavour, taste, relish, pleasure, essential property, extract, or essence'. So *rasa* in the first place means 'juice', and juice is liquid, flowing, has no fixed form. And freedom or *vimutti* is like that. It is not fixed or definite, not conditioned. On the contrary, it is absolute and unconditioned. And the Dharma-Vinaya, being pervaded by the taste of freedom, is likewise an uninterrupted flow of spiritual and transcendental states. It may crystallize into different teachings, practices, and so on, but it is not to be identified with them; it remains an uninterrupted flow.

Rasa means not only 'juice', but also 'taste'; and taste is a matter of direct experience. So the taste of freedom as an all-pervading quality of the Dharma-Vinaya is a direct, personal experience of freedom. If you practise the Dharma-Vinaya you will yourself become free.

Another expression offered to translate *rasa* is 'special quality'. The direct experience of freedom is the special quality of the Dharma-Vinaya, i.e. the quality by which you can recognize it. If it doesn't have this quality it isn't the Dharma-Vinaya, just as if something doesn't taste sweet it can't be sugar.

This brings us to yet another aspect of the meaning of *rasa*. That special quality of the Dharma-Vinaya gives it its distinctive 'flavour'. With practice we begin to appreciate this flavour, even to relish it: we begin to take pleasure in it, and to enjoy it. And so we find that *rasa* means also 'relish' and 'pleasure'.

Furthermore, *rasa* means 'essential property'. The experience of freedom is an essential property of the Dharma-Vinaya, and there is no Dharma-Vinaya without it. Whatever else you may have, if you don't have the experience of freedom you don't have the Dharma-Vinaya. Finally, *rasa* means 'extract' or 'essence'. If you were able to take the mighty ocean of the Dharma-Vinaya and distil it, if you were able to boil it down and condense it into a single drop, that drop would be freedom, or *vimutti*.

If we were then to visualize an image of that quintessential spirit, we would begin with the image of space or the image of the usual way we perceive space: the sky, infinite in extent, deep blue in colour, and perfectly pure. In the midst of this image there would be another image: a figure flying through the sky. It is a naked, red figure, a female figure. Her long black hair is streaming out behind her, her face is uplifted in ecstasy, and there is a smile on her lips. She is what is known in Buddhist tradition as the dakini or 'lady of space', the embodiment of the spiritual energy of the Buddha. She is absolutely free: free to fly in any direction – north, south, east, west, the zenith, and the nadir. She is free, even, to remain still. Hers is the liberty of infinite space. She enjoys the Taste of Freedom.

THE PATH OF REGULAR STEPS AND
THE PATH OF IRREGULAR STEPS

In RECENT YEARS the whole character of Buddhism in the West has radically and crucially changed. Buddhists today are likely to be much more deeply and wholeheartedly involved in the actual practice of Buddhism than they would have been before. They are much more concerned with the application of the Dharma – the teaching of the Buddha – to all aspects of their lives. Thus this radical and crucial change is essentially a change on the level of the individual Buddhist.

As you put an ever greater effort into following the Path, changes take place in your being and consciousness, and because of these changes you begin to see things differently. What was formerly important becomes unimportant, and vice versa. Such radical change may bring problems to be confronted; but as your Buddhist life simultaneously broadens and deepens, a sublime range of opportunities opens up before you. Not only that: as you actually follow the Path taught by the Buddha – as you *become* that Path – you begin to understand its nature more and more deeply and clearly.

You begin to see that within the one great central Path there are a number of alternative pathways to follow, or rather, that there are different ways of following the Path – some, perhaps, more helpful than others. In particular, you begin to appreciate the importance for your whole future spiritual development of the absolutely basic distinction between the path of regular steps and the path of irregular steps.

This distinction is a very ancient one. It goes back to sixth-century China, to the great Chinese teacher Chih-i, who was the virtual founder of one of the greatest of all Buddhist schools – though so far rather neglected by Western Buddhists – the T'ien-T'ai School. Besides producing important works of scholarship, Chih-i founded monasteries and preached the Dharma widely. By reason of his profound spiritual attainments he was able to attract an extraordinarily large number of disciples, and these he addressed from time to time, commenting upon the scriptures, speaking about the spiritual life, and especially, it seems, giving instruction on meditation. In the course of his discourses on meditation, many of which have come down to us, Chih-i spoke of meditation by regular steps, of meditation by irregular steps, and also of meditation without any steps at all.

When one mentions the third kind of meditation people usually become rather interested. They are not at all interested in meditation by regular steps, which sounds rather dull and prosaic. Meditation by irregular steps appeals to them quite a bit. But what really captivates and fascinates them is the idea of 'meditation without any steps at all', which means that one attains Enlightenment instantaneously by means of one phrase or even one word.

Unfortunately, people are usually attracted to this kind of meditation entirely for the wrong reasons; and at the risk of disappointing some readers we shall not give it any further consideration here. However, this still leaves us with more than enough to chew over, because Chih-i's distinction between meditation by regular steps and meditation by irregular steps is applicable not only to the practice of meditation but to the practice and experience of the whole spiritual path, in all its stages and all its aspects.

The fact that one can approach the Path, or the spiritual life, either by way of regular steps or by way of irregular steps is well understood in the Buddhist East, even though the two ways are not always differentiated in these terms. However, in Western Buddhist circles it is only recently that people have begun to appreciate the importance of the distinction between them – or even mention it. Perhaps the reason for this is that we have only recently reached the point where such a distinction becomes meaningful and helpful and even, I may say, necessary if we are to make further progress.

What then is the path of regular steps? What is the path of irregular steps? In attempting to answer these questions I propose to be a little irregular myself and deal with the second path first.

THE PATH OF IRREGULAR STEPS

When we look at Buddhism in the West today, the first thing that we see is books – hundreds of books – about Buddhism. This is the most conspicuous feature of Buddhism in the West. We see big books and small books, little pamphlets from the East and lavishly illustrated volumes from leading publishing houses in London and New York. We see simple, popular introductions to Buddhism, even books for children, and we see works of pure and daunting scholarship. We see books on Theravada, books on Mahayana, and of course books on Zen and the Tantra. We see books written by Buddhists of various persuasions, books written by non-Buddhists, books written by anti-Buddhists, and books written by all sorts of people who do not know *what* they are. Some of these books are original works, the product of much independent thought and study, while others are translations from Sanskrit, Pali, Chinese, Japanese, and so on. Altogether, there are thousands upon thousands of books with a connection of one sort or another with Buddhism.

If we are young and enthusiastic, and have lots of time, we start trying to read them all – or at least as many as we can of the better-known ones. Some of us may even get around to reading the Buddhist scriptures as well. And as we start to get an impression of Buddhism through our miscellaneous reading we also start forming ideas about it. These ideas tend to be very confused. If one approaches Buddhism through books one is almost bound to start off with confused ideas, so much so that we do not even begin to realize how confused we are until perhaps years afterwards – if indeed we ever do. But meanwhile, if we do enough reading, it is possible to make the big mistake of thinking that we understand Buddhism.

Then if we are not careful we may be tempted, after a few years, to share our understanding – in other words, our confusion – with other people. We start writing and speaking on Buddhism and in this way become quite well known: we may even have people sitting at our feet and drinking in our words of wisdom. We may be asked to speak on the radio, or appear on TV, and with a little luck we may even be invited to 'represent Buddhism' – whatever that may mean – at some interreligious gathering. But, all this time, what is really the position?

The position is that, quite literally, we do not understand Buddhism at all. It is not that we have a limited or partial grasp of Buddhism. The position is that if we think we understand Buddhism, we do not understand it at all.

When we understand a thing – whether we really understand it or just think we do – we become in some sense superior to that thing. Understanding means appropriating; it means taking the subject of one's knowledge into oneself, making it part of oneself, making it one's own. Thus we speak in terms of 'mastering' a subject: mastering accountancy, or mastering mathematics. And so we speak, or at least think – or even half-think – of mastering Buddhism. In this way the idea we have that we might understand or master Buddhism precludes the possibility of looking up to it, of feeling towards Buddhism, towards the Dharma, any real devotion or reverence. In 'mastering' the subject we have completely misunderstood it.

This kind of attitude is not new, and it is by no means confined to modern Western Buddhists. It has been widespread in the Western world for quite a long time. We find Samuel Taylor Coleridge, the great poet and thinker, complaining about it a hundred and fifty years ago (of course, within a Christian context) in the following terms: 'There is now no reverence for any thing; and the reason is, that men possess conceptions only, and all their knowledge is conceptional only. Now as, to conceive, is a work of the mere understanding, and as all that can be conceived may be comprehended, it is impossible that a man should reverence that, to which he must always feel something in himself superior. If it were possible to conceive God in a strict sense, that is, as we conceive of a horse or a tree, even God himself could not excite any reverence....' And reverence, Coleridge goes on to say, 'is only due from man, and, indeed, only excitable in man, towards ideal truths, which are always mysteries to the understanding, for the same reason that the motion of my finger behind my back is a mystery to you now – your eyes not being made for seeing through my body.' (*Table-Talk*: 15 May 1833.)

At about the same time as Coleridge was delivering himself of these sentiments, an even greater poet and thinker was saying much the same thing, though rather more briefly. In his *Maxims and Reflections* Goethe writes: 'The finest achievement for men of thought is to have fathomed the fathomable, and quietly to revere the unfathomable.'

It is this quiet revering of the unfathomable, of that which, in Buddhist terminology, is *atakkavachara* or beyond the reach of thought – beyond the reach of understanding and conception – that until recently has been so lacking among Western Buddhists. We have been much too quick to 'understand', much too ready to speak, even about the unfathomable – in fact, *especially* about the unfathomable.

This is not altogether our fault. To a great extent it is the result of the situation in which we find ourselves. Amongst the mass of published material available to us – amongst so many translations of ancient Buddhist texts – there is much that is extremely advanced. Some of the great Mahayana sutras, for example, are addressed to disciples of a high degree of spiritual development, as is made evident in their opening scenes. They begin with the Buddha seated in the midst of a great concourse of disciples, perhaps in some heaven or archetypal realm. All around him are arahants and great bodhisattvas, even irreversible bodhisattvas, that is, bodhisattvas who cannot regress from the ideal of supreme Buddhahood and who have, as it were, nirvana in the palm of their hand. The sublime teachings that the Buddha proceeds to give are addressed to such beings as these – beings who exist on a level of spirituality beyond all that we can conceive or imagine.

Being able to possess paperback translations of such sutras, it is perhaps easy for us to imagine that we can master their contents just as we can master the contents of any other paperback. We may tend then to adopt a cool, knowledgeable, even patronizing attitude towards Buddhism. Some of us may even think it unnecessary to call ourselves Buddhists at all – after all, we have 'gone beyond' all that. We may even look down somewhat on those simple-minded folk in the West who actually choose to call themselves Buddhists, who actually pay their respects to images of the Buddha, who actually offer flowers and light candles, and who actually try to observe the precepts.

We may think our lofty, detached attitude more advanced, but the truth is that it is simply superficial – a theoretical approach without any roots in genuine reverence, faith, and devotion. This shallow, purely mental approach, devoid of all devotion, of all 'quiet revering of the unfathomable', has generally characterized Buddhism in the West until comparatively recently. Indeed, there is still a strong tendency among Western Buddhists to pick and choose from the teachings 'on offer', not according to their own real spiritual needs but according to subjective and superficial whims and fancies. We like this bit, but not that bit. We are happy with the idea of karma, say, but we don't like the idea of rebirth. Or you find people being very much drawn by the doctrine of *anatta* (for some reason or other, the idea that they do not have a soul or a self seems rather to attract some people) but at the same time finding the thought of nirvana rather depressing.

Then, of course, likes and dislikes often change. For a while one may be very much into Zen, because one rather likes the idea that one is already a Buddha, already 'there', and that there is nothing to do. It seems to make life a lot easier: one does not have to practise anything, apparently, or give up anything. But eventually one gets rather bored with being a Buddha, so one starts getting into the Tantra; and Tantra, of course, immediately conjures up visions of sex, and one starts getting into the yoga of sex (theoretically, of course). In this sort of way one can browse and dabble for years.

Every one of us has experienced these difficulties in some degree or another, but still, a number of Western Buddhists do get around, in the end, to practising Buddhism. At a liberal estimate – based simply on personal experience – perhaps one in twenty Western Buddhists moves on and actually tries to practise Buddhism. Eventually the realization dawns that Buddhism is not just a collection of interesting ideas – not just a philosophy, not just something to think about. One tumbles to the fact that Buddhism is something to be applied, even something to be experienced.

Unfortunately, so strong is the force of conditioning and habit that even when one starts trying to practise Buddhism the same old pattern of picking and choosing, the same shallow, appropriative theorizing, persists. To see how this happens, we could take the case of an imaginary Buddhist called, say, John. He is twenty-four, and has been interested in Buddhism since he was twelve. Let us say that John is a bookish young man and has read all the standard authors on all aspects of Buddhism. You name a book on Buddhism and the chances are that John has read it. At last, after all that reading, it occurs to him that there might be more to Buddhism than reading about it, and he finds his way to a meditation class, where he learns, week by week, a technique of concentrating the mind. He gets on quite well, so much so that he can maintain a pleasurable experience of integrated concentration for ten minutes or so at a time, quite regularly.

But after two or three months he starts finding the whole thing rather pointless and boring. Nothing much seems to be happening. He just gets into a nice, concentrated state. There are no wonderful visions, no revelations, no divine voices speaking to him. He is beginning to lose interest altogether when he is lucky enough to hear about a wonderful new meditation teacher whom not many people know about because he has only recently arrived in the West. John finds that this teacher has all the unmistakable hallmarks of an authentic guru: a compassionate smile, a mellifluous voice, a penetrating gaze, and a wonderful beard. The first thing the teacher tells John is that he should forget whatever he has previously learned about meditation. It was all wrong. His previous teachers did not know the first thing about meditation. This naturally comes as a bit of a shock, and John feels rather disoriented; but anyway, he starts practising the new method of meditation with the new teacher and gets on quite well. In fact, he gets on about as well as he had done before, with the old method: neither better nor worse.

Unfortunately, after two months a rather serious setback occurs. The wonderful new teacher disappears. Not in the magical sense; John just goes along to the class one evening and finds that he is not there. Some people say he has gone back to India. Others say he has gone to America. There are different reports. Poor John is left high and dry, and doesn't know what to do.

However, he meets someone who introduces him to a kind of Sufi group. He finds the people there quite sociable, quite friendly;

but he does not get anything out of the teaching. In fact there isn't any teaching as such, because as far as this particular group is concerned, everything is one. So back he goes to Buddhism: or rather, back to reading books about Buddhism.

One day he happens to read a book about Buddhism and vegetarianism. 'That's very interesting,' he thinks, 'Buddhists go some way to avoid causing harm to living beings by the simple expedient of not eating meat. I never realized that before. Also, I see that they preserve their mindfulness by not indulging in alcohol. I had not thought of that either. In fact, Buddhists try to avoid doing quite a number of things.' This aspect of Buddhism had not struck him before. He has been so preoccupied with Buddhist philosophy, so preoccupied with the meaning of Emptiness and the One Mind, that it has not occurred to him until now that there might be quite simple, practical things to do, or precepts to observe.

In other words, John begins to see that there is an ethical side to Buddhism. Formerly he had not had time for anything so elementary as that, but now he starts thinking about it quite seriously, and actually starts trying, rather gingerly, to observe at least a few of the precepts. He gives up meat, stops drinking and smoking, and tries very hard not to tell lies or even to exaggerate. In his growing enthusiasm he starts becoming a bit puritanical. He starts carrying these things too far. But he is sincere, and as a result of his observance of the precepts he starts feeling like practising meditation again. Unfortunately, there are no wonderful new teachers around, so back he goes to his old class, which is still carrying on. Again he gets into regular practice, does quite well, and after some months is able to sit for over an hour without too much difficulty.

One day a rather strange thing happens. John arrives for the weekly class late and exhausted after a heavy day. He is not at all in the mood for meditation: he thinks that since he is tired it is going to be rather a waste of time. But he goes anyway and he sits. Without any warning, after he has sat for a few minutes, he finds himself in a completely different state of consciousness. How he got into it he does not know. He is hardly aware of his body. Everything seems very bright and luminous, very buoyant. He feels fresh, without any trace of tiredness, as though some inexhaustible spring was welling up within him. It is as though his whole being is expanding, and he begins to glimpse things he has never glimpsed before, despite all his reading of books and his intellectual understanding. A great wave of bliss descends upon him. He feels as he has never felt before, and never thought to feel. How long he remains in this completely different state of consciousness he does not know. It may be ten minutes, or even half an hour.

Whatever it is, the experience has a very profound effect on John. He *knows* now that there is some higher state of consciousness, of being. It is not just words, not just theory, any more. It is not just something he has read in a book. He feels that at last some progress has been made; and he is so impressed, so elated, that he starts thinking of becoming a monk, going to the East, leading an ascetic life, and so on. He even feels he can gain Enlightenment quite soon.

Elated and pleased with himself, he becomes a little more expansive, a little more outward-going than before – and at this point Mara starts taking an interest in John. Mara is the demonic being who symbolizes all forces inimical to the Truth, to the Dharma, and he has not bothered about John before. After all, it has not been necessary, since some of the books John has been reading have been doing Mara's work for him.

Now there is a girl who has been coming to the meditation class for a few weeks. She is a well-meaning girl, but she is destined to be the innocent instrument of John's downfall. Being rather shy, John has never spoken to her, but in his present elated, expansive mood he loses his shyness. He speaks to her that week, the following week they become friends, and to cut a not very long story short John falls violently in love with her. But the girl, perverse creature that she is, does not fall in love with him. She is in love with somebody else. Poor John! He cannot eat, he cannot sleep, and of course he cannot meditate. He forgets all about his wonderful experience. It is as though it has never been.

We all experience something like this from time to time. You get into a wonderful, exalted state, and think that you are going to have no more trouble, no more problems. 'Now I really know what it's all about,' you say, 'I shall never be such a fool again.' But a few days – even a few hours – later, you are back where you were before, apparently. It is like that with John. It is as though he has never had that experience of a higher state of consciousness in the first place. He forgets all about Buddhism. He does not go to the meditation class any more because he cannot bear to meet the girl. In fact, he feels like committing suicide.

But one day someone invites him to a party. Now John does not usually go to parties. As I said, he has become a bit puritanical. But he is feeling so miserable that he accepts, goes to the party, and gets drunk. Bang goes a precept, of course, and he wakes up the next morning with a terrible headache. But John is young, and youth is resilient. Eventually he gets over his disappointment. Our latest news of him is that he is no longer trying to observe the precepts, and has given up meditation, but he is busy reading books on Tantric Buddhism, and thinking of taking up the study of Tibetan.

It is very easy to smile and shake one's head at John's confusion, to feel a bit superior. But of course he has just been following the path of irregular steps; and this is what we all do, and perhaps have to do, at least for a time. We practise now this meditation and now that, and then maybe we do not meditate at all for a while. We go through a period of observing the precepts quite strictly, we are even quite puritanical; but then we do not bother about them for a while. One day we feel like giving everything up, going off to the East and becoming a monk; but the next day we start wondering whether Buddhism is really the thing for us at all. Thus we follow the path of irregular steps – and sometimes our steps are very irregular indeed.

Not so long ago there was very little Buddhism in the West, in any form, whether books or otherwise. Now, one might say that there is almost too much. There are so many books, so many practices, so many teachers, so many schools to choose from. There is such a bewildering confusion and profusion of forms in which Buddhism is presented. In our excitement and greed we snatch first at this and then at that, sampling a bit here and a bit there, like a greedy child in a sweet shop. We are in the transcendental sweet shop of Buddhism, with all these beautiful spiritual goodies around us. And so we reach for this and scoop up a handful of that: Zen, Tantra, Theravada; ethics strict and ethics liberal; meditation plain and meditation colourful. We just grab – that, it has to be said, is what our approach to Buddhism amounts to at times. But all the same we do make some progress in this way. The path of irregular steps is still a path, and it does give us some experience of Buddhism.

But only up to a point. As we follow the path of irregular steps we find, sooner or later, that we are slowing down. We seem to be up against an invisible obstacle. Apparently in a sort of spiritual doldrums, we are going through the motions, but nothing is happening: we don't seem to be getting anywhere. At this point a radical change is called for. We need to make not just another change of direction within the path of irregular steps, but a more fundamental transition: a transition from the path of irregular steps to the path of regular steps.

Now why is this? And what, anyway, is the distinction between these two 'paths'? To answer these questions we must first understand the nature of the Path in general, the Path which leads from the *samsara*, the round of mundane, conditioned existence, to *nirvana*, the 'realm' of unconditioned being, the Path from unenlightened humanity to the Enlightened humanity of the Buddha.

THE THREEFOLD PATH

The Buddhist Path is traditionally divided into three successive stages: the stage of *shila* or morality, the stage of *samadhi* or meditation, and the stage of *prajna* or wisdom. Though there are other ways of dividing – and even subdividing – the Path, this threefold division remains the most important and the most fundamental.

Shila, morality, is simply skilful action: action which benefits oneself, which helps one to grow and develop; and action which benefits others too, which helps them also to grow and develop. Not that *shila* is a matter of external action divorced from mental attitude; it is both the mental attitude and the mode of behaviour in which that attitude naturally expresses itself. Thus *shila* is skilful action in the sense that it is action arising from certain skilful mental states, especially states of love, generosity, peace, and contentment. It is, indeed, everything one does out of these skilful mental states. That, essentially, is what morality or ethics in Buddhism comprises: actions expressive of skilful mental states.

Samadhi, usually translated 'meditation', is a word with many different meanings on a number of different levels. First of all it consists in the gathering together of all one's scattered energies into a single focus. Most of the time our energies are divided; they take different directions; they are unintegrated. So first of all we have to integrate them. This does not mean forcibly concentrating on a particular point; it means bringing together all our energies, both conscious and unconscious, and harmonizing them in a natural and spontaneous manner. Thus concentration, in the sense of the complete unification of one's psychospiritual energies, is the first grade or level of *samadhi*.

Next, *samadhi* consists in the experience of progressively higher states of consciousness – states extending into what are called the *dhyanas* or superconscious states. In these states we transcend the body (in the sense of physical awareness) and also, eventually, the mind (in the sense of discursive mental activity). We also experience bliss, peace, joy, and ecstasy (but not transcendental insight, since we are still within *samsara*, still within the realm of the mundane).

Finally, *samadhi* includes the development of such supernormal powers of the mind as telepathy, clairvoyance, clairaudience, and the recollection of one's previous existences. However, 'supernormal' does not mean 'supernatural': when these powers arise in the course of meditation, they do so quite naturally and spontaneously.

The last stage of the threefold Path is *prajna* or wisdom. This consists in direct insight into, or personal contact with, the Truth or Reality. At first it occurs only momentarily, like a sudden flash of lightning that, on a dark night, lights up the landscape just for an instant. As the flashes of insight become more frequent, however, and more continuous, they eventually become a steady beam of light that is capable of penetrating as it were into the very depths of Reality.

When fully developed, this wisdom or insight is what we call *bodhi* or Enlightenment – though at that level it is not to be spoken of in exclusively cognitive terms. At that level we also have to speak of it in terms of love and compassion or, rather, in terms of the transcendental counterpart of the emotions which we usually designate by those names.

THE PATH OF REGULAR STEPS

Thus the Path, which constitutes the main theme of Buddhism on the practical side, is divided into these three great stages of morality, meditation, and wisdom. The division is not an arbitrary one: the stages are no mere chalk marks, but are inherent in the Path itself, and represent natural stages in the spiritual and transcendental growth of the individual. As such they resemble stages in the growth of a plant: from the seed comes forth a little shoot, which grows into a stem, from which leaves and finally buds and flowers are produced.

Of course we must not push an analogy of this sort too far. The whole process of the flower's growth is unconscious. The flower does not have to decide whether to grow or not; nature 'decides' for it. But in the case of a human being spiritual development is conscious and deliberate, and by its very nature must be so. We are dependent for our further growth on our own individual, personal effort – though this is not a one-sided, egoistic, straining wilfulness, but the growth and development, in awareness, of the whole being.

A more satisfactory analogy for spiritual development from this point of view (though it doesn't work so well as an illustration of a development from within) is that of the construction of a house or any multi-storey building. First you lay the foundation, then build the first storey, then the second, and so on, and finally you put on the roof. You cannot reverse the sequence, because it is determined by the nature of the structure itself.

The stages of the path of regular steps correspond to various Buddhist teachings; and different teachings pertain to different stages of the Path, that is, to different stages of spiritual and transcendental development. When we practise the Dharma we should therefore practise those teachings which correspond to the stage of development we have actually reached – and reached not mentally or theoretically but with our whole being. This is the traditional method, or at least the predominant traditional method.

So first you practise morality: you observe the precepts. In doing so, you gradually become a thoroughly ethical individual, both inwardly and outwardly – this may take several years. Then, when your ethical individuality has been established relatively firmly, you take up the practice of concentration: you learn to tame the unruly wandering mind, and to concentrate at will on any object for any length of time – which may take several more years. Then, very slowly, you start raising your level of consciousness. You experience the first *dhyana*, the second *dhyana*, and so on, gradually training yourself not just to touch them but even to dwell in these superconscious states. Finally, perhaps after many years of endeavour, you direct your purified, elevated, and sublimely concentrated mind, together with the integrated energies of your whole being, to the contemplation of Reality itself. This is the path of regular steps. Progress is systematic; you consolidate each stage of the Path before proceeding to the next one.

By contrast, in treading the path of irregular steps one starts practising on the basis of a more or less mental or theoretical grasp of the Dharma (and a confused and incomplete grasp at that). Usually, I am afraid, in the West, one begins without a teacher; and one does not start practising those teachings which correspond to the stage of development one has actually reached, because one does not know what stage one is at anyway. One starts practising in a way that is immediately and superficially appealing – one starts practising, perhaps, what appeals to one's vanity. One might, for instance, start practising the Perfection of Wisdom.

Now it is not absolutely impossible, even for an absolute beginner – even on the basis of a purely theoretical understanding of the subject – to practise the Perfection of Wisdom. After all, the seed of Buddhahood is there, however deeply hidden. Deep down, an affinity with the Perfection of Wisdom is there. One may succeed, to a very slight extent, by sheer force of the egoistic will, in holding oneself, just for an instant, at a level of concentration where one gets just a glimpse of the Perfection of Wisdom, an experience, however fleeting, of the Void.

However, one will not be able to keep it up. One will sink back from it, and there will even be a reaction – a reaction from one's whole being or consciousness, which is, as a whole, simply not at that level and not ready to practise the Perfection of Wisdom. So one has to go back. One has to practise ethics and meditation, develop higher states of consciousness, and, in this way, create a firm basis from which to practise the Perfection of Wisdom effectively.

So following the path of irregular steps usually involves forcing the process of spiritual development. It is like trying to make a plant grow by forcibly opening the buds with one's fingers, or like building a house without foundations. Sooner or later we discover that it cannot be done. Instead of pulling open the buds one has to water the roots. One doesn't start building anything until one has dug the foundations. As Buddhists, the flower that we want to see blooming is the thousand-petalled lotus itself, so plenty of water is needed. The tower we want to build is the tower that reaches up into the very heavens, so a very firm foundation is required.

To state the matter axiomatically, we may say that a higher stage of the Path cannot be developed even to a moderate extent before a lower stage of the Path has been developed in its fullness. This is the basic principle. If we want to experience the higher stage, or higher level, with any intensity or any permanence, we must first perfect the lower stage. There is no other way. This is why, sooner or later, we have to make the transition from the path of irregular steps to the path of regular steps. And this transition means, basically, going back in order to go forward.

MAKING THE TRANSITION

We have already noted that the character of Western Buddhism has recently undergone a radical change. We can now begin to see in what that change consists. It consists, essentially, in a transition from the path of irregular steps to the path of regular steps. More and more Western Buddhists are beginning to realize that a shallow, superficial approach to the Dharma – an irregular, unsystematic, improperly based practice of the Path – is not enough. They have begun to realize that we have to go back to the beginning, back, one might almost say, to the spiritual kindergarten, to start learning our spiritual ABC.

But how far back does this mean? One could say: back to morality – back to basics. Or one could say: back to the Hinayana, back to basic Buddhism; put aside Tibetan Buddhism, put aside the Tantra and Zen, and get back to the Theravada. But in fact we have to go back to something even more fundamental than morality, even more basic than the Hinayana. We have to go back to the Three Jewels.

We have to sit or kneel with hands together, and go for Refuge, saying '*Buddham saranam gacchami, Dhammam saranam gacchami, Sangham saranam gacchami*. To the Buddha for Refuge I go, to the Dharma for Refuge I go, to the Sangha for Refuge I go.' This is where Buddhism really begins. This is the root, the foundation, the absolute bedrock of our spiritual life. This is how we really start practising the path – by going for Refuge.

Thus we make – or begin to make – the transition from the path of irregular steps to the path of regular steps. We go for Refuge to the Buddha: we commit ourselves to the ideal of human Enlightenment, and we make it the aim and object of our lives to become Enlightened even as the Buddha was Enlightened. We go for Refuge to the Dharma: we commit ourselves to the systematic, wholehearted practice of the Path to Enlightenment. And we go for Refuge to the Sangha: we commit ourselves to cultivating the spiritual friendship of those who are treading, or who have trodden, the Path to Enlightenment.

Going for Refuge is the basic declaration of commitment to the Buddhist Path. It is the quintessential act of the path of regular steps, an act of commitment by the whole person. It is, therefore, at once basic and momentous. In fact, if one goes for Refuge to the Three Jewels, and if, as an expression of one's determination to follow the path of regular steps, one also undertakes to observe a greater or smaller number of moral precepts, and if one moreover does all this openly and publicly, in the traditional manner, then this Going for Refuge, or commitment, is what we call ordination.

Usually it is assumed that ordination means monastic ordination, that is, we think it means becoming a *bhikkhu*, or *gelong*. But this is a great misconception and it is high time we sorted it out. Monastic ordination is only one kind of ordination. The Sanskrit word for ordination is *samvara* – literally a 'binding' – and we therefore speak of *upasaka-samvara*, *bhikkhu-samvara*, and even *bodhisattva-samvara*, as well as the feminine equivalents of the first two – *upasika-samvara* and *bhikkhuni-samvara*. In other words we speak of lay ordination, monastic ordination, and even bodhisattva ordination. But all three are ordinations, the same word, *samvara*, being applied to each of them.

Upasaka/upasika, bhikkhu/bhikkhuni, and bodhisattva all equally go for Refuge – the bodhisattva, perhaps, in a deeper sense than the other two. All three commit themselves to the Three Jewels. Any difference between them is simply as regards the number and, in the case of the bodhisattva, the kind of precepts observed. So what the monk and the layman, the bhikkhu and the upasaka, have in common is far more important than what they do not have in common. What they have in common is the Three Jewels, or the Three Refuges, and for the Buddhist nothing can be more important than that. Thus the real line of demarcation is not between monks and laymen but, properly speaking, between those who have gone for Refuge and those who have not.

The sangha or spiritual community in the ordinary sense of the term (as distinct from the Sangha in the sense of all the bodhisattvas, arahants, and other great saints), is simply and straightforwardly made up of all those who have gone for Refuge. The distinction between the monk and layman is, therefore, a distinction *within* the sangha. We may even go so far as to say that so far as the sangha is concerned the distinction between the monk and layman probably owes more to the social and cultural condition of India at the time of the Buddha than to the intrinsic nature of the Dharma itself. In which case, it is a distinction that may or may not be relevant to the development of Buddhism in the West.

Unfortunately, the supreme, overriding importance of Going for Refuge is not always appreciated. Only too often it is regarded as a rather ordinary thing. For example, one afternoon a good many years ago now, a young man came to see me and said 'I am quite interested in Buddhism: I have read a few books, and done a little meditation. But I don't want to commit myself to Buddhism; I think I am more interested in worldly life. So would you please just give me the Refuges and Precepts?' I had to explain that his request was self-contradictory. Commitment is what Going for Refuge means. There is no point in 'taking' the Refuges if one is not prepared to commit oneself; one would be merely repeating the words. The young man could not understand this and went away disappointed and dissatisfied. Subsequently I heard that he had 'gone for Refuge' with a more accommodating teacher and then continued with his worldly life.

This sort of misunderstanding is not, it should be said, peculiar to the West. In fact it has spread to the West from the East. In the East Buddhism has had a very long and a very glorious history, of which we can be justly proud. During the two-thousand-five-hundred years of its existence, Buddhism has produced great art and great literature, great systems of thought and, above all, great lives. But it would be idle to pretend that serious degeneration has not taken place in some areas, and we can see instances of this in the matter of the 'Going for Refuge'. Originally, Going for Refuge represented a profound spiritual experience: you were moved to the very depths of your being, as we know was the case with the people who went for Refuge to the Buddha himself when he was alive. It was a matter of wholehearted commitment – wholehearted surrender – to the Three Jewels and to the spiritual life. Nowadays, unfortunately, in many parts of the Buddhist East, the whole concept and experience of Going for Refuge has been devalued. The absolute bedrock of Buddhism appears as just something that you recite, in a dead language, on festive occasions.

It is easy to see how this has come about. After all, if the term Buddhist means anything it means 'one who goes for Refuge'; and yet in some parts of the East the whole population considers itself Buddhist, just as until recently the whole population of Britain considered itself Christian. For such people the term 'Buddhist' does not necessarily imply a vigorous commitment to genuine spiritual values. So Going for Refuge – or 'taking the Refuges' – has become something one does in order simply to accord oneself the denominational label of 'Buddhist'.

In some Buddhist countries, therefore, we have a rather curious situation. When one does want to commit oneself to the spiritual life and take Buddhism seriously – when really one wants to go for Refuge – one thinks not in terms of going for Refuge, but in terms of becoming a monk (or nun, though that is largely impossible these days). Even though one's commitment to the Three Jewels may not include a heartfelt desire to express that commitment through taking the step of monastic ordination, one still thinks in terms of joining a monastery and putting on the yellow robe. Meanwhile, the vast majority of the population formally 'go for Refuge' to signify only a nominal loyalty to the Three Jewels. The result is that the most fundamental act of a Buddhist is drained of significance, while the committed spiritual life comes to be more or less identified with a monastic life that is itself, all too often, only nominally monastic.

One can understand how this situation has come about in the East; there are all sorts of historical reasons for it. But in the West there is no excuse whatsoever for perpetuating what is in fact a very serious distortion of Buddhism. Unfortunately, visiting Buddhist teachers from the East have rarely perceived this distortion or understood what ordination and Going for Refuge really mean. If you show any sign of genuine interest in Buddhism they want to make you a monk – sometimes on the spot – because to them ordination means monastic ordination. But as we have

already seen, ordination essentially means Going for Refuge, and
Going for Refuge means ordination, or commitment.

As Western Buddhists make the great transition from the path of
irregular steps to the path of regular steps – as they start becoming
ordained – we don't have to imagine people rushing off to the East
and donning robes. What we can expect to see is a form of ordination for men and women in the West that reflects the true meaning
of Buddhist ordination. And one situation at least where this can
be found at present is in the Friends of the Western Buddhist Order,
the FWBO. The heart of this organization is the Western Buddhist
Order, founded in 1968, which is a community of people who have
committed themselves to the spiritual life, to the Three Jewels, who
have, individually and in fellowship with one another, gone for
Refuge.

The Order is called 'Western' because it has arisen in the West,
under the conditions of a secularized and industrialized society. It
is called 'Buddhist' because it derives its inspiration ultimately
from the teachings and the example of Gautama the Buddha and
all the great Enlightened saints and sages and spiritual masters
who are his spiritual descendants. It is an 'Order' because it
recognizes – in the midst of a world which is in many ways difficult
and destructive – the great value of spiritual fellowship in treading
the Path; and because it seeks to create a reservoir of spiritual
energy on which all may draw and from which all can benefit; and
because, above all, it realizes the importance of the distinction
between the path of regular steps and the path of irregular steps.

ENLIGHTENMENT AS EXPERIENCE AND AS NON-EXPERIENCE

BUDDHISM CONSISTS of two things: a path, or way; and a goal, or objective.

The Path has been described in various ways, according to context. It is delineated as the Noble (or Holy) Eightfold Path – a path of eight stages, or more accurately, eight members or factors. It is outlined as the Path of the Six (or Ten) *Paramitas* or Perfections. It is also defined as the Middle Way, the path between and above extremes. These are only some of the ways in which it is described.

As for the goal, this is described – very provisionally – as Buddhahood, in the sense of Supreme Perfect Enlightenment. This goal can also be conceptualized in various ways. It can be seen as supreme wisdom, or absolute gnosis, or insight into things 'as they really are'; as the plenitude of compassion, pouring out on all sentient beings simultaneously; and as infinite spiritual – even transcendental – energy radiating in all directions. It can also be conceived in terms of complete and utter purity, a purity which is not only clear of the stain of evil but beyond the polarity of good and evil. Enlightenment can be cognized in these and many other ways. In particular we can think of it as an experience, as *the* experience, even: the culminating experience or, if you like, the experience to end all experiences.

But what is an 'experience' anyway? We use the term often enough, but what do we mean by it? In a sense any and every object of perception, whether physical or mental, whether sense-based or abstract, is an experience of some kind. But usually we like to distinguish experience from thought – or at least from abstract or conceptual thought. Basically, experience is a matter of perception and feeling; it means the actual living through of an event, the actual – as we say – *experiencing* of it, not just the 'experience' of looking at it or contemplating it. Experience also suggests 'real life' as distinct from ideal or imaginary life or existence.

Enlightenment as experience means, therefore, Enlightenment as something you actually perceive, actually feel. It is, in the words of Wordsworth in his poem 'Tintern Abbey', 'felt in the blood, and felt along the heart'. It is felt in the nerves, felt in the bone. It is not just abstractly thought and speculated about, or imagined and fantasized about; it is something that you live through. However, if you do live through the experience of Enlightenment, you do so in a way that marks it uniquely apart from any other experience.

With any other experience you come out at the other end, so to speak, whether intact or (to some extent) not intact. But you do not come out at the other end of the experience of Enlightenment. There is no other end. Maybe there is an end of 'you', but that is another matter. 'You' do not come out at the other end. What we can say is that your life continues, after you have experienced Enlightenment, not as you but as Enlightenment; or, rather, that your life becomes a continuing part of Enlightenment itself.

But how did we come to think of Enlightenment in this way – as experience? For we must not think, just because we have become used to it, that this is the natural, the inevitable, and the only way of thinking about it. Indeed, it is a rather odd way of thinking; and there are alternative ways.

Indian Buddhism does not refer to Enlightenment as experience. In the Pali scriptures of the Theravada School, some portions of which evidently come close to describing the way the Buddha originally taught, there is no reference to Enlightenment as an experience. The very early Buddhists did not, so far as we know, think of Enlightenment in that way at all. Experience was implied, but it was not stated in so many words: indeed, there was no equivalent expression in Pali.

In a later text, one of the greatest of the Mahayana sutras, the *Lankavatara*, we find an expression that its translator into English, D.T. Suzuki, renders as 'the experience of noble wisdom'. So it would seem that there was a change of emphasis between the earliest Pali texts and this relatively late sutra, compiled in its present form probably not less than eight hundred years after the time of the Buddha. One might even say that its emphasis on experience, or on something corresponding to what we now call experience, reflects developments taking place in India analogous to certain developments which took in the West very much later.

However, the word 'experience' in Suzuki's English version of the *Lankavatara* is actually a very approximate, not to say loose, translation of the Sanskrit term *gatigochara*. Also from the *Lankavatara* we have the term *pratyatmagochara*, which Suzuki renders as 'inner realization'. Again, this term resembles, in its meaning, something close to what we understand by the idea of experience without doing so closely enough to call it such. Thus even if we accept that the *Lankavatara* does, in a way, speak of Enlightenment in terms of experience, it does so in a rather indirect and equivocal manner (as neither *gatigochara* or *pratyatmagochara* can be translated with any real precision by the word 'experience').

In Pali and Sanskrit it is as difficult to speak of Enlightenment as experience (in the current sense of the term) as it is to express another notion current amongst Western Buddhists but apparently unknown to ancient Buddhists, which is that 'all life is one'. To say that all life is one may be a justifiable interpretation or reinterpretation of Buddhist teaching, but you can't put it back into either Pali or Sanskrit. It represents a quite different mode of expression

– a mode of expression which is the product of a modern, Western way of thinking.

If you do translate 'Enlightenment is an experience' or 'All life is one' back into Pali or Sanskrit you then become involved not in translating but in reinterpreting the sutras, in rethinking and, if you like, in re-experiencing them or making them new – which according to some schools of Buddhism is one of the things you must not do. *Navakata*, as they call it, or making new, is for them equivalent to heresy.

So speaking of Enlightenment as experience is a mode of expression peculiar to our own particular mode of experience – to use the very word we are discussing. Seeing things in terms of experience is part of the way in which we have come generally to regard religion – and, indeed, life itself.

RELIGION SEEN AS EXPERIENCE

Now how is this? This is no place for a detailed historical analysis but in brief we can say that up to the time of the Reformation in the sixteenth century European religion was a very much richer and more complex phenomenon than it subsequently became. Up to that time religion – consisting almost entirely of a single strand of Christianity which had superseded earlier beliefs – presented quite a number of different aspects. There was doctrine, especially in the form of theology and scholastic philosophy; there was ethics; there was ritual, sacrament, and liturgy; there were festivals, celebrations, and pageants; there were social institutions, folk customs, law (i.e. canon law), myth, legend, mysticism, asceticism – even marvels and miracles. Up to the time of the Reformation, all these things went to make up religion. We can even include art – painting, sculpture, architecture, and music – all of which, in their most ambitious and refined forms, were mainly or at least ostensibly concerned with, and celebrated, religion as the dominant system of values. So in religion we had, at one time, a many-splendoured thing indeed, something very rich, very complex, and very inspiring.

But the great synthesis broke down. With the Reformation came a change, especially in the Protestant parts of Europe. There wasn't any one Christian doctrine any more, and as the number of conflicting and competing versions of the 'one true faith' proliferated, doctrine became much more rigid. Myth and legend and all the more colourful elements – in the Protestant countries especially – gradually disappeared, while ritual dwindled to a ghost of its former splendid self. In some areas, ritual was banished altogether. The fine arts became more and more secularized. The church was separated from the state. Religion was divorced from secular life and became more and more a matter of private morality and personal feeling.

In England this trend was intensified during the Victorian period, when the traditional religious doctrine of the origin of the universe and of mankind was very much undermined by discoveries in the fields of geology and biology – particularly by Darwin's theory of evolution. For many good, serious-minded, and sincere people the Christian religion became more and more intellectually untenable. For some, like Matthew Arnold, religion became simply 'morality tinged with emotion', as he calls it. The morality was often little more than social conformity, and the emotion little more than a feeling of nostalgia for a lost faith. For others, religion became not morality tinged with emotion but emotion tinged with morality and, as the decades went by, that emotion became less and less tinged with morality.

It was at this point, roughly one hundred years ago, that Buddhism first made a real impact in the West. If we wanted a date, we could fix upon 1879, the year of the publication of Sir Edwin Arnold's beautiful and justly celebrated poem on the life of the Buddha, *The Light of Asia*. And as was inevitable, Buddhism came to be regarded in much the same way that Christianity was, either as a system of ethics, or as a particular kind of religious sentiment or feeling, that is, as an experience.

Thus one could have predicted that Buddhism would not, at that stage, be taken very seriously as a 'doctrine' or 'philosophy' (for want of a better term) – and nor was it. The depths of Buddhist thought were not plumbed at that time. They did not even begin to be plumbed, and we are far from doing so even today, a hundred years later.

Nor should it have been difficult to foresee how people would take to Buddhist myth and legend. The long and hopeless struggle of Christian myth or legend to dress up as historical fact had put people in no mood for what they would naturally imagine might be more of the same from Buddhism. As for rituals, festivals, and social institutions, and all the more popular and colourful developments of Buddhism, these would have been regarded as being simply out of the question even by the very, very few in Europe who, in those days, thought of themselves as Buddhists. After all (they might have argued) had not the Buddha, good Protestant that he was, condemned rites and ceremonies as a fetter?

On the basis of this initial reception of Buddhism in the West as a religion of ethics or of 'experience', one should also have been able to forecast, at the end of the nineteenth century, which forms of Buddhism would be the most popular in the West during the first half of the twentieth century. These were, of course, Theravada and Zen – Theravada as representing a code of ethics, and Zen as representing experience. Thus it was that the way we in the West have come to regard Buddhism is the result of the way in which we have come, almost insensibly, and over hundreds of years, to regard religion in general.

LIFE SEEN AS EXPERIENCE

The way we regard religion – even unconsciously – ties in closely with the way we regard life itself, that is, the organized life of the human community, or social life in the widest sense, along with its various aspects, political, economic, cultural, and domestic. The question we need to ask, however, is perhaps not so much how we feel about Life – Life with a capital L – as whether many of us feel very much about life at all. Do most of us, to be honest, feel anything more than simply confused and bewildered?

Life has indeed become so complicated that sometimes it seems as though we have become caught up in a vast machine, too big and complex for us to understand or do anything about. We are so well-informed about whatever is happening all over the world, all the time, and yet even when these events affect our own lives deeply and intimately, we are apparently powerless to do anything about them. The juggernaut of world events rolls on. Even if the wheels are crushing the life out of us, it seems that we can do nothing. It is easy to feel helpless, impotent, frustrated.

At the same time, life can often seem to be a very dull and routine affair. We rumble or creep along tracks which were laid down for us even before we were born – perhaps before even our parents were born. One hardly needs to describe where the familiar journey takes us. First comes school and, of course, nobody asks to be sent to school. After school comes some combination of work and marriage, mortgage and children, promotion (which means more work) redundancy and retirement, followed inevitably by death. This is what life means for most people, and apparently there is no alternative. The wheel has trapped us, and rolls on and on.

This predicament is vividly illustrated in a very striking painting by Burne-Jones, called 'The Wheel of Fortune' (though 'The Wheel of Misfortune' would have been a better title). It depicts an enormous wheel turned by a rather stern-looking woman, and on this inexorably turning wheel are strapped a variety of helpless (male) figures. It presents a pattern of meaning that many, perhaps, would identify as being applicable to their own lives.

Crucial to the perception that we have of the meaning of our lives is, usually, work – work in the sense of gainful employment. We devote more time and energy to work in this sense than to any other single activity – perhaps with the exception of sleep. Yet work is generally perceived as something dull, repetitive, exhausting, and boring. Few find any joy or sense of fulfilment in it; few find a feeling of creativity or any real outlet for their energies. People may be bursting with energy, but they can rarely put it into their work even if they have work; it is not needed there. And if there is no creative outlet for these energies, such people feel frustrated, impotent, and, deep down, very resentful. But again, only too often, they have not the resources to express that resentment. The expression of resentment is a luxury that very few workers can afford. In any case, if they work for a multinational conglomerate, who is there to vent it on? Understandably, some of those who have little to lose express their resentment in criminal activities, even in criminal violence.

Without an outlet for our energies, we gradually lose contact with our feelings; when we lose contact with our feelings we lose contact with ourselves; and when we lose contact with ourselves we lose contact with life. We become dull, tired, mechanical, dead. We become walking corpses. We all know, more or less, what this is like; from time to time we have seen it in ourselves, to some extent, and we have seen it in others. The great poet and visionary, William Blake, saw it nearly two hundred years ago, at the time of the grimy dawn of the Industrial Revolution. He says:

> I wander thro' each charter'd street,
> Near where the charter'd Thames does flow,
> And mark in every face I meet
> Marks of weakness, marks of woe.

We can see these same 'marks of weakness, marks of woe' on the faces of people in the streets, in cars, on buses and trains today. The only difference, two hundred years after Blake, is that those marks are now, if anything, more deeply scored.

But of course human beings are very resilient; the energy is still there, however distorted or deeply buried. We don't always take things lying down – and quite rightly so. We look about us for something to relieve the sense of frustration, of numbness. We look for some excitement, for something that will give us a bit of a thrill: something that will make us feel more alive; something that will take us out of ourselves; something that will make us forget everything – for a while anyway.

So we turn to food, to sex, to alcohol and other drugs, to the television set, and to the passive consumption of music and art and literature – with an occasional surrender to the ever-present lure of a more expensive dress, a faster car, a more powerful motorbike, or a smaller computer. For an extra boost of stimulation, we plug in to the tribal excitement of a crowd at a football match, or even the bloodlust of the foxhounds on the hunting field. In its extreme form this tendency will seek fulfilment in violence and sadism. In our search for relief from boredom we turn to all sorts of things, from the sublime to the sordid, from Beethoven to bingo.

Not all the above examples are, of course, bad things in themselves. It is the use we make of them that is questionable – that can be neurotic or, in the more traditional Buddhist terminology, 'unskilful'. In fact anything we undertake simply to relieve boredom and frustration will, in the long run, make us feel more empty, more frustrated, more drained, more exhausted, than ever. Unfortunately, this self-defeating exercise is, as we know, a universal phenomenon of modern life.

So we tend to feel rather ambivalent about life. On the one hand we find it oppressive, frustrating, burdensome, stultifying. But on the other we expect from it something that will alleviate that frustration, something compensatory: an *experience*.

We can now begin to see how the way we regard religion links up with the way we regard life. There is a common emphasis, eventually, on experience (in the wider sense of the term). This is why it is almost inevitable that we should think of Enlightenment too in terms of experience. For purely historical reasons we are predisposed to think of religion, and of Enlightenment, in terms of experience. And on account of the general nature of modern life we are on the lookout for experience anyway; we are on the lookout for *the* experience that will transport us beyond that life, even beyond ourselves.

So not only are we in a position of quite naturally thinking in terms of religion as experience; we also have a neurotic need for experience to alleviate our mundane boredom and frustration. Hence we come to place a great emphasis on experience, and crave experience; and that emphasis is unhealthy because we are, very often, alienated from experience.

ENLIGHTENMENT SEEN AS EXPERIENCE

Many of those who turn for their favourite brand of experience to the various spiritual traditions of the world are very tightly locked in to this neurotic craving for – and at the same time alienation from – experience. They have already tired of at least some of the more usual forms of distraction. In some cases they may even have dropped out of ordinary social and economic life altogether, possibly because they were too weak or sensitive to cope. With nowhere and nothing to turn to – with even, perhaps, no one to turn to – they are willing to try anything to relieve this dull, aching inner void.

So they start haunting spiritual groups and workshops, religious and occult bookshops, meditation classes and initiations. They take up astrology, magic, and witchcraft – white witchcraft, black witchcraft, and probably a sort of grey witchcraft too. They take up occultism, the Cabbala, the Vedanta, Sufism, Taoism, Buddhism. They take up anything that might take them out of themselves, anything that might give some shadow of meaning to their lives; anything that might give them an experience.

Not long after I returned to England in the 1960s having spent twenty years or so in India, I happened to visit a well-known occult and oriental bookshop in London. Rather to my surprise it was full of people, even though it was a weekday, and I saw that all these people were absolutely oblivious to one another. They all had their eyes glued – not to say riveted – to the bookshelves. As I entered the shop I also noticed that the whole place was pervaded by a heavy, oppressive atmosphere which I felt I had encountered before – though where and on what occasion eluded me.

And then it came to me. Two years earlier I had been in a large department store in an English seaside town, and in the food section, standing around just like waxworks, were a number of elderly women with shopping baskets. They all stood quite motionless gazing fixedly at the food, and they gazed at it with what can only be described as dull, reptilian greed. It was this same greed that I saw and felt there in the bookshop. It was the same greed for pabulum, for something to feed on, the same neurotic craving for experience.

There is, however, a crucial distinction to be drawn between the neurotic craving for higher spiritual experience, and a genuine *aspiration* for such experience. The distinction is essentially between wanting to acquire and wanting to attain. Attainment is the result of a gradual growth, an extension of our own being and consciousness into higher levels and new dimensions, an extension which is, in a sense, a natural process. By contrast, acquisition in this context is the attempted appropriation of the higher level, or of the new dimension, by and for ourselves *as we are now*, an unnatural and unrealistic process – unrealistic, because it cannot possibly succeed.

Attainment is like the growth, the gradual unfoldment and flowering, of a healthy plant. But acquisition is taking to ourselves something which we ourselves haven't produced, like a neglected plant with a stolen bloom – or even a plastic flower – tied on to its sapless stem. It is as if we were to tie a lifeless simulacrum of the Buddha's own golden flower, the flower of Enlightenment, on to the barren branches of our own lives. So attainment is a matter of growing, acquisition a matter of grabbing – a sort of smash-and-grab raid on the Absolute.

Nor is this grabbing attitude towards spiritual experiences the worst kind of acquisitive attitude. There is, after all, something to be said for people who seize what they want with both hands. One can't help grudgingly admiring the boldness of the bank robber, for instance, in one's weaker moments. Much more unhealthy, much more hopeless, is an attitude of passive expectancy: lying back, mouth wide open, waiting for the experience to be fed to one, claiming transcendental experience as if one had some kind of inalienable right to it, and resenting the idea that anyone, let alone oneself, should be excluded from this experience simply because they do not measure up to it. This idea that the universe owes us not just a living, but an experience – even *the* experience – is a particularly disabling example of the false positions we can get into when we project the notion of Enlightenment as experience.

I have taken an extreme, even exaggerated, look at these false positions in order to throw into stark relief what we are really looking for when we turn for guidance to Eastern spiritual traditions – particularly to Buddhism. The purpose of the exercise is a very practical one. After all, the cultural conditioning that emphasizes feeling and experience is a hard fact of all our lives. So is the modern world with its high-speed travel, mass information, and controls and regulations. We cannot avoid being affected to a greater or a lesser extent by the world in which we live. We *are* the modern world, each of us to a certain extent, so that each of us is alienated to a certain extent – alienated from ourselves, and alienated from life – and we are all therefore, whether we want to or not, looking for compensations.

So we approach Buddhism with very mixed motives, partly healthy and partly unhealthy. No doubt in principle each and every one of us would wish to think in terms of attainment, of growth, but only too often we behave in terms of acquisition – we grab. We need to be aware of the whole underlying tendency to think of the goal as an experience, because the consequences of thinking in this way are potentially disastrous for the spiritual life. Before moving on to consider Enlightenment in terms of non-experience, then, let us first be clear about what these dangers are.

If our attitude is one of neurotic craving, if we are passive and demanding, and if we expect to be *given* a spiritual experience, then our expectation will take one or more of three specific forms. We will expect the experience to come from some*where*, or from some*one*, or from some*thing*. On account of this threefold expectation we may fall victim to three different syndromes which we can describe as pseudo-spiritual exoticism, pseudo-spiritual projection, and pseudo-spiritual technism.

PSEUDO-SPIRITUAL EXOTICISM

Pseudo-spiritual exoticism means that we expect the great experience to come from far away – the further away the better. Ideally, it should come from outer space, but if that is not possible then it should at least come from the East – if, that is, if we live in the West. If we live in the East and suffer from this same syndrome, we expect the great experience to come from the West. It seems that young Japanese Buddhists, for example, have been known to sing Protestant Christian hymns in their temple because they sounded so exotic.

This is more or less what we do in the West. Buddhism, for instance, is of oriental origin, historically speaking, and it generally comes to us dressed in oriental garb, not to say oriental ornaments. It comes to us wearing an Indian, or a Japanese, or a Tibetan style of dress, and we are naturally fascinated by this strange, beautiful, and glamorous apparel. The problem is that we may well be more interested in the outfit than in what is inside – than in Buddhism itself as a universally valid spiritual teaching which is in its essence neither of the East nor of the West. We even think that Buddhism *is* the costume it comes in. We may even think that if only we could get hold of a little scrap of this dress – a little relic, as it were – then we would have something essentially Buddhist, something authentically spiritual that will magically transform our lives.

The basic assumption that supports this idea is that the East is good and the West is bad. Some people even talk about 'the Eastern mind' as if it were constitutionally different from 'the Western mind' – the Eastern mind being a highly spiritual mind, and the Western mind a grossly materialistic mind. But this is, of course, a complete travesty of the facts.

Sad to say, some Eastern teachers, or perhaps I should say certain persons coming from the East and purporting to teach, encourage this sort of attitude. It makes them feel good and sometimes, to put it bluntly, even flatters their nationalistic prejudices. They too, in the course of centuries, have come to think that the dress is Buddhism, or that the dress is the Vedanta, or that the dress is Sufism, as the case may be.

Of course there are highly spiritual teachings in the East, and of course we can learn from those teachings, and should be immensely grateful that we have been brought into contact with them. But our concern with them should be a concern with the truth, not a concern with the exotic.

PSEUDO-SPIRITUAL PROJECTION

In the case of pseudo-spiritual projection we expect the experience to come not just from somewhere else but from some*one* else. Personal relationships are, as we know, much more intense – much more 'loaded' – than non-personal ones, and hence this particular syndrome is much more dangerous than the last. The person from whom we expect the experience is, of course, the great guru. We ourselves have to do nothing. All we have to do, miserable wretches that we are, is to believe in him, believe that he can give us the experience.

Naturally, the experience can't be given by just an ordinary man, not even by an ordinary, run-of-the-mill guru. It can be given only by a very great guru indeed – a living Buddha, a fully realized master, the embodiment or incarnation of God, or at least the personal representative of God on earth. Unless we believe in him in this way we don't get our experience. Not only that, but because we so much need to believe in this particular person, we cannot entertain a doubt, we cannot tolerate criticism of him. And criticism is here understood as including any disinclination to accept him as God or as a fully Enlightened master. Everybody has got to believe in him just as we do. If necessary they must be made to believe. It's all for their own good, anyway.

But how do you know that the great guru is God, or a Buddha, or Enlightened? Well, it's quite simple. You know because he says so. In this way a very dangerous situation develops. The bigger the claims made by the great guru, the more likely it is that the kind of vulnerable people who *need* to believe him *will* believe him. Since there is no shortage of such people nowadays, this kind of self-inflated guru quickly rakes together quite a large following.

A different case is when an ordinary guru is turned into a great guru by his own followers. They see more in him than is actually there. He may be a good man, even a spiritual man, but they project on to him qualities that he does not objectively possess, and sometimes he succumbs to their projections. Should he not succumb the followers are often very disappointed. They feel rather let down. They may even become angry if he refuses to accept their projections, or to allow them to build him up into a great guru. So they leave him. They continue their search for the great guru, for someone who will give them the experience they want – or at least promise to give it.

All these things have happened – they do happen – and it is all very sad. One cannot help feeling, it must be said, deeply ashamed sometimes of what has been done and is being done in the name of Eastern religions, even in the name of Buddhism – ashamed of the way in which the weak-minded and the credulous have been exploited by the globe-trotting gurus of the twentieth century. One can even find in fringe newspapers, 'alternative lifestyle' magazines, and the like, all kinds of such gurus advertising themselves like so many brands of soap powder, all making tremendous claims, all asking for support, for belief.

If we are going to be on our guard against this sort of thing, we have to see where the source of the trouble lies. It is not so much in the great guru: it is in ourselves, in our own weakness and passivity, our own wish to have things done for us, our own neurotic craving for experience – an experience that someone else must give us as a free gift. And we need to see as well where our real solutions are going to come from: again, they lie within us, in our own potential to grow into the experience ourselves, as a result of our own individual, responsible effort and exertion.

PSEUDO-SPIRITUAL TECHNISM

Pseudo-spiritual technism consists in attaching exaggerated importance to particular methods of practice, especially methods of meditation, or concentration techniques. We think that if we can only find the one right, infallible method or technique, it will automatically give us the experience. Or else we believe that we have actually found such a method or technique, and then of course we become very dogmatic and intolerant about it. All other methods are dismissed as worthless. Only our own technique, only the method to which we ourselves have recourse, is the right and efficacious one.

Such pseudo-spiritual technism may be encountered within almost any school, but for myself I have in the past encountered it particularly among followers of what used to be called Vipassana meditation – i.e. the New Burman Satipatthana method – and also in connection with Zen. Some practitioners of these methods have tended, sad to say, to be rather contemptuous of other forms of meditation practice, thinking that if one is not practising *their* favoured method then one is not meditating at all.

This neurotic overvaluing of one particular technique is to forget that in Buddhism, especially, there are many different methods of meditation, many different concentration techniques, every single one of which has been tested for centuries and every single one of which works – provided one practises it. One method may be more suited to a particular temperament, or a particular stage of development, than another, but we can never say that any one method is intrinsically better than any other.

ENLIGHTENMENT AS NON-EXPERIENCE

These three syndromes are the unwholesome consequences of thinking of religion, and thinking of Enlightenment, too literally and exclusively in terms of experience. But what is the alternative? What may be prescribed to relieve us of them? To begin with, we can try a simple but radical experiment: just to stop thinking in terms of experience for a while and instead to start thinking in terms of *non*-experience; to start thinking of Enlightenment itself, even, as non-experience.

This way of thinking can be traced in the Pali scriptures. In the *Dhammapada*, for instance, we encounter the saying '*Nibbanam paramam sukham*: nirvana is the supreme bliss.' The implication is that there is a difference between worldly bliss, including the highest heavenly bliss, and supreme or nirvanic bliss. So where does this difference lie?

The essential characteristic of worldly bliss is that it depends on contact between the sense-organs and the mind on the one hand, and their respective physical and mental objects on the other. It depends on some kind of contact between a subject and an object. Worldly bliss depends, in short, on experience; it is a form of experience. But nirvanic bliss is not so dependent; it does not arise in dependence upon any sort of contact, and is not the product of contact. When all contacts cease, that is nirvana, that is the bliss of nirvana. Hence nirvana is not an experience, and we can only describe it as a non-experience. Nirvana is the experience you have when you've stopped experiencing.

Nirvana as non-experience is also described in terms of cessation (*nirodha*), that is, in terms of the entire, complete, remainderless cessation of the conditioned. What this means so far as we are concerned is the cessation of experience – because all our experience is conditioned. The cessation of the conditioned means the cessation of all our experience because conditioned experience is the only kind of experience we know. We do not know any other kind of experience. We do not know unconditioned experience. For us, unconditioned experience is a contradiction in terms, a logical impossibility. Therefore, to the extent that we think of nirvana, or of Enlightenment, as cessation, we must think of it as non-experience.

But here we stand on the Everest of Buddhism, where the air is very clear but very cold. Perhaps we had better go a little lower down, and try to find a more positive, more concrete way of approaching Enlightenment as non-experience – a way that is more helpful to the genuine fulfilment of our real human needs. We need, in short, to think not only of Enlightenment as non-experience, but also of religion, of spiritual development, of the Buddhist Path or Way, as non-experience. I am going to suggest three ways of approaching the Buddhist Path as non-experience – all very closely linked. These are: seeing it in terms of *growth*; seeing it in terms of *work*; and seeing it in terms of *duty*.

SEEING BUDDHISM IN TERMS OF GROWTH

The primary image of growth or growing is that of the plant, an image which figures very prominently in traditional Buddhism. To take a central instance, the Buddha's vision of humanity as he sat under the bodhi tree after the Enlightenment (if Enlightenment has an 'after') was as a great bed of lotuses in various stages of development. Looking out over the world he saw that some people were sunk in the mud, so to speak, some were halfway to the surface, while others had risen above the water and stood drinking in the sunlight with open petals. The Buddha saw all living beings in this way: as plants – as lotuses – at different stages of development.

This great vision has stayed with Buddhism throughout its two-thousand-five-hundred years of history. There have been many great philosophical developments, some of them, in all conscience, dry and abstract enough. There has been a good deal of scholasticism and, later on, plenty of formalism. But Buddhism has never forgotten the Buddha's great vision of that bed of lotuses standing there in the early morning sunlight. It has never forgotten that image of growth, of growing; and the image has assumed many different forms.

It has become, for instance, the Lotus Throne, that many-petalled throne on which innumerable Buddhas and transcendental bodhisattvas sit and meditate, teach, and radiate light. It has become the great lotus-like Refuge Tree, with its central trunk and four great branches, each terminating in an enormous many-petalled lotus flower on which sit Buddhas, bodhisattvas, arahants, gurus, yidams, and dakinis. Perhaps above all, we think of its appearance in the *White Lotus Sutra*'s parable of the herbs and plants, also known as the parable of the rain cloud. In this parable the Buddha sees humanity not just as lotuses but as plants of many different kinds: trees, shrubs, creepers, grasses, herbs. When the rain of the Dharma falls the 'plants' all grow, but they grow – and here is the parable's distinctive teaching – in their own way, each according to its own individual nature.

There is no need to multiply examples. Suffice it to say that they all bear witness to the advantages in thinking of Buddhism not so much in terms of experience as in terms of growth, seeing ourselves drinking in the Dharma as a plant drinks in the rain. Growth is a total thing: the whole of us is – or should be – growing all the time. There is no question of our working our way up to growth. The process is absolutely continuous. Growth doesn't lie only at the end of the process; if we are working our way up we are growing. All such effort is growth.

We may say that the spiritual life, the Path, is like the plant, and Enlightenment, the goal, is like the flower. In one sense, of course, the flower is separate from the plant. However, in another sense the flower is part of the plant, the natural product of the plant, the culmination of its growth. It cannot be stuck on to the plant from outside. It cannot appear before the plant has reached the stage of development when the flower *naturally* comes forth. Whether it seems to us premature or late, the flower always appears at the appropriate time.

So likewise with the flower of Enlightenment. You can reach the goal of Enlightenment only by following the Path. You cannot grab Enlightenment as if it existed apart from the following of the Path. Enlightenment is no more separate from the Path than the flower is separate from the plant.

The image of the plant and the flower is a beautiful and appropriate one, but like all images it has its limitations. A flower, after all, fades and loses its petals, which is hardly the case with the culmination of the spiritual life. Therefore, if we want the image to carry its meaning further, we have to stretch our imagination in order to expand and develop the image.

So firstly, we have to imagine a flower that does not fade, whose petals do not fall. We have to imagine a flower that remains when all the rest of the plant, the stalk and the leaves, have dropped away. Or else, perhaps, we should imagine that the whole plant has become the flower, which seems to float, suspended, in the sky. Moreover, like other flowers, this flower seeds new plants, which produce flowers in their turn which also remain floating in the sky. And as this process has no end we have to imagine it continuing to eternity, and then we must imagine the whole of space becoming filled with flowers. This meditative vision of the whole of space filled with a vast network of great golden lotus flowers – a network expanding to infinity in all directions – is what the Buddhist life is really like.

But it is time we came down to earth, and back to a sense of space and time. It is time we came down from the flower to the plant, back to the individual struggling to grow, back to ourselves. As the parable of the herbs and plants reminds us, the plant needs rain – but it needs quite a number of other things too, if it is to grow. It needs sunshine, it needs, perhaps, wind; it needs soil, with everything soil contains; it needs even so humble a thing as manure; and maybe a little pruning from time to time, or protection from pests or wild animals. It may even need – if it is not so proud as to disdain the aid – a stick to support it for a while. In other words, growth depends on a whole complex of favourable conditions. All of which brings us to a very important point indeed: that we need to establish the process of growth within a wider and ever wider context. And this implies a fuller and richer conception of Buddhism itself.

Buddhism is not just ethics, not just meditation. It is a lot more than these two things, great and important as they are. Buddhism is a doctrine, a teaching, even a philosophy. It is a whole series of great myths. It is a body of legends. It is a complex of social institutions. It is a regular pattern of festivals and celebrations. It is a treasure-house of the arts. It is ritual. It is work. As Buddhists we need to be nourished by all these things, though we may need more of some than of others, depending on the kind of plant we are.

Buddhism is also a whole range of different schools and movements and traditions. And we need the nourishment of all of them. We don't need them in the rather mutually-exclusive, occasionally sectarian form in which they exist in at least some parts of the East. We need what is essential in them all – what is fundamental, living, and nourishing in them all – as we try to grow in the light of Buddhism here in the West.

Perhaps the Triyana Buddhism of Tibet offers a model in this respect. There is probably a hopeful sign for Western Buddhism in the fact that the dry bones of contemporary Theravada and the cold tea leaves of modern Zen have now been replaced in popular favour by the rich symbolism of Tibetan Buddhism (leaving aside the element of pseudo-spiritual exoticism in that appeal). However, the T'ien T'ai Buddhism of China (continued in Japan as the Tendai School) perhaps offers us an even better model than does Tibetan Buddhism, being not *Triyana* but *Ekayana:* not three ways but, in principle, one.

SEEING BUDDHISM IN TERMS OF WORK

Let us begin by making it clear that work, here, is not to be confused with gainful employment, with wage-slavery. Work is the productive expenditure of energy. This is the true, the noble meaning of the word 'work'. Work in this sense is the exact opposite of passively waiting for an experience. It is the direct opposite of the neurotic craving for experience. It is a joyful and creative thing. Work is productive in the sense of helping us to grow.

The most productive kind of work, the most productive expenditure of energy, is work for the Dharma – if possible, full-time work. And work for the Dharma does not just mean giving lectures and taking classes on Buddhism. Not everybody is equipped to do that. There is also bricklaying for the Dharma, cooking and cleaning for the Dharma, painting ceilings for the Dharma: a productive expenditure of energy through which we grow, and grow rapidly. For work of this sort, the more of us there are, the wider the context we need.

That wider context is the sangha, or spiritual community, in the widest sense; that is, the sangha as consisting not just of those who are technically and officially monks, but of all those who are treading the Path of the Buddha. We began by reminding ourselves that Buddhism consisted of two things: the Goal and the Path – the Buddha and the Dharma. But in fact Buddhism consists also of this third thing: the sangha or spiritual community of all those who are seeking to attain the Goal, who are treading the Path, who are growing, and who are working together for the Dharma.

SEEING BUDDHISM IN TERMS OF DUTY

Duty is not a word that goes down very well with many people. It lost its popular appeal somewhere in the mud of Flanders in the First World War. However, any adult learns to accept duties of one kind or another, even at the basic level of, say, having a duty to one's children. So how do we define duty? what is one's duty?

To this question the great German poet and thinker Goethe answered: 'The claims of the day.' (Eckermann, *Conversations with Goethe*, 1936.) There is just one modification one would wish to make to this magisterial definition. If one said 'the claims of the *larger* day,' one would bring out the necessary distinction between lesser claims on us and greater claims. Goethe goes on: 'And how can a man learn to know himself? He can learn to know himself never by reflecting, but by doing. Endeavour to do your duty and you will at once know what lies in you.'

What then is the duty of a Buddhist – of one who has gone for Refuge? What is our duty as members of the spiritual community? It is simply to work – productively, joyfully, creatively. It is to do whatever can reasonably – or even in some circumstances unreasonably – be expected of us in the situation in which we find ourselves. If we do our duty as Buddhists – if we work as Buddhists, work for the Dharma – we shall know ourselves as Buddhists. In fact we shall eventually know ourselves as Buddhas. We will gain Enlightenment: gain Enlightenment as experience and as non-experience – and both, and neither.

The Windhorse symbolizes the energy of the enlightened mind carrying the Three Jewels – the Buddha, the Dharma, and the Sangha – to all sentient beings.

Buddhism is one of the fastest growing spiritual traditions in the Western world. Throughout its 2,500-year history, it has always succeeded in adapting its mode of expression to suit whatever culture it has encountered.

Windhorse Publications aims to continue this tradition as Buddhism comes to the West. Today's Westerners are heirs to the entire Buddhist tradition, free to draw instruction and inspiration from all the many schools and branches. Windhorse publishes works by authors who not only understand the Buddhist tradition but are also familiar with Western culture and the Western mind.

For orders and catalogues contact

WINDHORSE PUBLICATIONS
11 PARK ROAD
BIRMINGHAM
B13 8AB
UK

Windhorse Publications is an arm of the Friends of the Western Buddhist Order, which has more than sixty centres on four continents. Through these centres, members of the Western Buddhist Order offer regular programmes of events for the general public and for more experienced students. These include meditation classes, public talks, study on Buddhist themes and texts, and 'bodywork' classes such as t'ai chi, yoga, and massage. The FWBO also runs several retreat centres and the Karuna Trust, a fundraising charity that supports social welfare projects in the slums and villages of India.

Many FWBO centres have residential spiritual communities and ethical businesses associated with them. Arts activities are encouraged too, as is the development of strong bonds of friendship between people who share the same ideals. In this way the FWBO is developing a unique approach to Buddhism, not simply as a set of techniques, less still as an exotic cultural interest, but as a creatively directed way of life for people living in the modern world.

If you would like more information about the FWBO please write to

LONDON BUDDHIST CENTRE   ARYALOKA
51 ROMAN ROAD   HEARTWOOD CIRCLE
LONDON   NEWMARKET
E2 OHU   NH 03857
UK   USA

ALSO FROM WINDHORSE

PARAMANANDA

CHANGE YOUR MIND: A PRACTICAL GUIDE TO BUDDHIST MEDITATION

Buddhism is based on the truth that, with effort, we can change the way we are. But how? Among the many methods Buddhism has to offer, meditation is the most direct. It is the art of getting to know one's own mind and learning to encourage what is best in us.

This is an accessible and thorough guide to meditation, based on traditional material but written in a light and modern style. Colourfully illustrated with anecdotes and tips from the author's experience as a meditator and teacher, it also offers refreshing inspiration to seasoned meditators.

208 pages, with photographs
ISBN 0 904766 81 0
£8.50/$16.95

SANGHARAKSHITA

A GUIDE TO THE BUDDHIST PATH

Which Buddhist teachings really matter? How does one begin to practise them in a systematic way? Without a guide one can easily get dispirited or lost.

In this highly readable anthology a leading Western Buddhist sorts out fact from myth, essence from cultural accident, to reveal the fundamental ideals and teachings of Buddhism. The result is a reliable map of the Buddhist path that anyone can follow.

Sangharakshita is an ideal companion on the path. As founder of a major Western Buddhist movement he has helped thousands of people to make an effective contact with the richness and beauty of the Buddha's teachings.

256 pages, with illustrations
ISBN 1 899579 04 4
£12.50/$24.95